SQUADRON LEADER
TOMMY BROOM DFC**

Plea
You
or b

C153651840

SQUADRON LEADER TOMMY BROOM DFC**

THE LEGENDARY PATHFINDER MOSQUITO NAVIGATOR

TOM PARRY EVANS

Pen & Sword
AVIATION

First published in this format in Great Britain in 2007
By Pen and Sword Aviation
An imprint of
Pen and Sword Books Ltd
47 Church Street
Barnsley
South Yorkshire
S70 2AS

ISBN 978 1 84415 649 8

A CIP record for this book is available from the British Library

First pubished by the author in 1999 as 'A Posset Lad'.

Printed and bound in England
by Biddles Ltd

Pen and Sword Books Ltd incorporates the imprints of Pen and Sword
Aviation, Pen and Sword Maritime, Pen and Sword Military, Wharncliffe
Local History, Pen and Sword Select, Pen and Sword Military Classics
and Leo Cooper.

For a complete list of Pen and Sword titles please contact
Pen and Sword Books Limited
47 Church Street, Barnsley, South Yorkshire, S70 2AS, England
E-mail: enquiries@pen-and-sword.co.uk
Website: www.pen-and-sword.co.uk

Acknowledgements

The writer acknowledges his debt to many people, but has cause to specially thank:

Tom Broom for being himself and for having been, many years ago, Tommy Broom;

Bert Metcalf for his art work and photography;

David Haigh for his invaluable help in producing the original publication;

Ms Christine Gregory and her colleagues at The Royal Air Force Museum at Hendon for their generosity in providing material free of charge for the original publication;

Dorothy Evans, my late wife, for her patience and understanding when the original publication was being researched.

Contents

Introduction

I can remember clearly, as if it were only yesterday, the one occasion when I saw my parents with tears in their eyes. We were listening to the 9 o'clock news on the wireless when the fall of Singapore was announced. I looked across the farmhouse hearth and a cold chill went through me when I saw them gazing tenderly at each other in an extraordinarily sad and knowing way. They seemed to sense that never again would they see their eldest son. Months later, we learned that Dewi had escaped on one of the last boats to leave Singapore for Sumatra. From there he crossed the narrow channel to Java where he boarded a ship bound for Colombo in Ceylon. He spent some time recuperating on the island before being posted to a squadron stationed on the Burmese front: his task there was to recover crashed planes from the surrounding jungle and, if possible, to repair them.

Three years went by. Towards the end of 1944, my mother was diagnosed with incurable cancer. My father immediately applied to the War Office seeking compassionate leave for George with a Royal Artillery coastal battery in Cornwall, for Esmond with the Royal Welch Fusiliers, for Winston with the Royal Artillery in Germany and for Dewi with the Royal Air Force in Burma. As the worldwide military situation was improving rapidly, the War Office responded generously and all four were granted leave. It took Dewi a long time to hitch lifts from Burma and he did not reach Blighty until nearly the end of April 1945. On the last lap of his journey – on the bus from Carmarthen to his home village of Porthyrhyd – an old acquaintance recognised him and greeted him with words of sympathy. That was how Dewi found out that our mother and father had been buried together a week earlier. In the time it had taken Dewi to travel from Burma, our father, also, had developed a fatal cancer. A week or so later, the war in Europe came to an end. Over sixty years have gone by since, but the memory of such bitter irony still moves me deeply and I weep again for my dear parents and Dewi.

Such family tragedies were experienced all over Britain. There is nothing more heart-rending to read than the simple inscriptions on a memorial erected in the churchyard at Tewkesbury Abbey. It was put up in the first place as a tribute to Major Bertram Cartland who was killed in action in France on 29 May 1918 within a few months of the end of the First World War. His widow was left on her own to bring up their two sons then aged eleven and five. Exactly twenty-two years later to the very day, on 29 May 1940, her younger son, Captain James Cartland, was killed on active service in France and, as if that hurt were not enough, on the very next day her eldest son, Major Ronald Cartland, suffered the same fate. Their mother, bereft of husband and sons, survived for another thirty-six years. When she died just before her hundredth birthday, the brief, dignified words of remembrance said of her, 'With courage, never to submit or yield.'

It is well nigh impossible for present generations to understand what happened so long ago or to appreciate the everyday horrors of the war years. Nor can they measure the vast courage of quite ordinary men and women, people now in their seventies, eighties and nineties who, in the days of their youth, faced danger and suffered sorrow so bravely.

Five years after the war ended, my wife and I settled in Portishead, and we made our home happily amongst such fine Somerset people. Though Britain was still trying to recover from the devastation of war, the 1950s were years of hope of better times to come and, indeed, in some ways they came. In other ways, perhaps, the community has deteriorated and there is no longer the same feeling of togetherness that we used to cherish so much. It is in this frame of mind that I am writing this account of a Portishead lad who brought honour to his village those long years ago, and whose story should be made known to today's younger generations, to whom the last war is, or was, but a part of their school history lessons.

In this new millennium, it will do us no harm to dwell on those supreme qualities of steadfastness, loyalty, courage and honour that were then so readily displayed.

Tom Evans
Summer 2007

CHAPTER ONE

Posset Born and Bred

Until about twenty years ago, Portishead was a small coastal town. It is situated in the north-west corner of the old county of Somerset, where the river Avon flows to swell the Severn into the Bristol Channel. As you pass by on the motorway to the West Country, you may catch a glimpse of its rooftops when you look across the Gordano Valley towards the new Severn Bridge. Perhaps because it is tucked away, until recently Portishead was similarly overlooked in travel books, yet the town and its countryside have a history and geography that are of more than passing interest.

On the crown of Naish Hill (you cross its lower slopes on the motorway) there is an old Celtic defensive ring known as Cadbury Camp, which may date back to the Bronze and Iron Ages some 2500 years ago. There is evidence of a much earlier settlement in the area, for during the digging of the Marine Lake in 1910 and in other chance excavations since, flint scrapers and knives of the Middle Stone Age and polished stone axes of the New Stone Age have been unearthed. Much later there was a substantial Roman occupation: second-century coins and pottery were found scattered in the remains of a villa excavated after a pipe-line had been dug through the grounds of Gordano School in the early 1960s. Portishead (Portesheve in 1086 and Portesheved in 1200) may well be derived from 'port' (Old English for harbour) and 'heafod' (Old English for headland), or it may have Romano-Celtic roots – 'porth' (port or gateway) and 'hafod' (summer habitation). This is a feasible interpretation for it is in the 'Land of Summer' that the paradise of Celtic Arthurian mythology, the Vale of Avalon, may be found. Maybe in times gone by, one certain way to achieve Paradise was to cross the Severn waters by coracle to Porth Hafod. Some writers have wondered whether Cadbury Camp may have served as an Arthurian stronghold,[1] one of his Camelots where he and his 'knights' camped during their guerrilla campaign against the Saxon hordes. A further mythological speculation is that the 'Wyvern' (the red dragon of Somerset) is akin to 'Y Ddraig Goch' (the red dragon of Cymru).

There is uncertainty about the origin of Gordano as well, a name that is happily exclusive to this region. In the thirteenth century, various documents referred to Gordenland, Gordeyn and Gordene. In her delightful book about the valley, Eve Wigan offered 'gar' or 'gore' (spearhead) – a triangular shape that matches that of the valley itself, and 'dene' (flat place) – a thoroughly adequate description of a valley that is but 20 feet or so above sea level. Some have drawn attention to 'Godwin's Land', a recognition that King Harold's family once owned the valley estates, whilst others have saluted Gunni the Dane who was a lord of the manor at Walton (or Welshton), and to whom we may be indebted for bequeathing us such an unique name as Gordano. Maybe it is derived from the Celtic 'gor-doi' (to cover completely), an accurate definition of the marshland that Gordano once was. Indeed, as a Cymro long resident in the delightful valley, I have a fanciful notion that the really old families of the Gordano villages (including Portishead) may be descendants of the Celts rather than of the Saxons, for the people seem to be blessed with a modest, gentle humour not usually associated with barbaric invaders! It is paradoxical that the Dark Ages of Saxon heathen-brutality came to be known, also, as the Age of Saints, that is, of Celtic Christian belief. Gildas was a hermit on Steepholm and Congar built a church at Congresbury believed to be the site of the first bishopric of Somerset. The Saxons, of course, brought with them their own language, but there are a few local geographical terms that can be traced back to their Celtic roots, words such as 'combe', 'Avon' and 'pill'. A pill is an inlet, a sort of miniature fjord without the cliffs.

The Saxons who came were perhaps attracted by the small, narrow natural harbour, the pill, a tidal creek navigable at high tide. They may have been the first to build a primitive sea-wall to save the valley from regular flooding. The Normans followed and, with their feudal society, organised a more stable settlement. There were two manors, at Court House and the Grange and, later, a third at Capenor. However, their existence did not signify that Portesheved was of any particular importance. The village was but a part of the Hundred of Portbury in the Shire of Somerset in the Earldom of Wessex. The lordships changed hands frequently during the Middle Ages, but in the seventeenth century the manor houses and their lands were acquired by the luxuriantly rich City of Bristol. It was about this time, also, that the fort on Battery Point, commanding the sea-lanes, was captured by the Parliamentarians. Within a fortnight or so, Prince Rupert was forced to surrender Bristol, so it may not be too far-fetched to claim that the capture of Portishead brought to an end the Civil War in the West Country.

As far as the common people were concerned, changes of greater significance occurred with the enclosing and the draining of the land in the eighteenth century. At that time, the Gordon family held sway, and was so influential that the 'Blew Anchor' was renamed 'The Gordon Arms'. In succeeding centuries it became the 'Anchor' and then, conforming to a foolish ruralising fashion, the 'Poacher'. The 'Blew Anchor' represented Portishead's affinity with the sea. There is not much doubt that smuggling was an important aspect of village life. It is said that there are few large houses built over 200 years ago that do not have substantial cellars! According to Eve Wigan, in the *Portishead Poor Rate Book* there are entries that emphasise the role of the sea and sailors in the history of the village.

In the nineteenth century, in order to enhance the value of its holdings, the City of Bristol decided to develop Portishead as a holiday resort. A hotel and a few lodging-houses were built and, to facilitate the expected holiday-makers, in 1867 a railway line was completed to connect the village to Bristol. Twelve years later, a proper dock was constructed where the pill was. Despite all this Victorian enthusiasm and despite its proximity to the great city, the village never developed into a seaside resort, partly because of its river-muddied coastline washed by the second highest tide in the world and partly, perhaps, because Posset people tended to be content with life as it was.

So, at the turn of the twentieth century, Portishead was a country village still, very likely better known to seafarers on their way up the Channel to Bristol than to other travellers. Most of the villagers were Somerset folk who spoke in the warm and kindly dialect of their county. This, one assumes, explains why the village became known in the outlying parishes as 'Pozey' or 'Posset', though to a stranger's ears 'Por-zed' would have been a more precise written translation of the spoken word. In fact, there is a story put about that a Londoner posted to the village during the war could not understand that Port Said should be so chilly and so English! It has been claimed that over the centuries there have been as many as seventeen different spellings of Portishead. Certainly, Emanuel Bowen was not too sure, for in his map of Somerset, dated 1760, he entered both Portshead and Porshut. Almost two centuries earlier, on his map dated 1575, Christopher Saxton marks the little promontory as Porshut Point.

Today, where Roath Road joins Slade Road, there is a patch of green where Rhondda Villas used to stand, and it is here that this story really starts, for it was at No. 2 that Thomas John Broom was born on 22 January 1914. Queen Victoria had died precisely thirteen years' earlier, but Victorian custom and morality still governed the conduct of ordinary people. Rules such as 'respect for authority' were held in high regard and, indeed, insisted upon by those who had power and who enjoyed the privilege of wielding it. It seemed as if the common folk were conditioned to have low expectations so that wealth and influence could be preserved for those who already possessed them. However, the more tender values of love, honour and generosity were nurtured mainly by Christian training, by precept in church and by example at home. In their everyday lives, people treated their fellows with considerable courtesy.

Very soon after Tom's birth, men and women all over Europe were driven to display some of their finest qualities when they were drawn into the conflicts of the First World War, and by the time Tom was four years old, the whole world had suffered in one way or another. By Armistice Day in 1918, there were 8,000,000 war dead, 6,000,000 civilian dead, and 21,000,000 wounded as evidence of people's willingness to suffer for what they believed to be just causes, and what they felt to be their duty to preserve national honour.

Tom's father, John Ashford Broom, served his King, Country and Empire faithfully. He was with the Army Medical Corps in France, stationed near Calais. When he returned to Old Posset to work again as a draper's assistant in Osmond and Tovey's shop (now, in

2007, Worthington's) he brought with him his Active Service New Testament with this message in it from Earl Roberts:

> *I ask you to put your trust in God. He will watch over you and strengthen you. You will find in this little book guidance when you are in health, comfort when you are in sickness, and strength when you are in adversity.*

In 1939, Mr Broom gave the Testament to Tom, and it is still in his proud possession. There is not much doubt that 'Service' was a family watchword. Mr Broom was a senior member of the St John Ambulance Brigade formed in the village, and a fellow member was Tom's younger brother, Bob. Despite his sober sense of duty, Mr Broom did not lack humour, and he would tell a story against himself with glee. One evening as he entered the Working Men"s Club, a village wag called out, 'Hello, Broomy.' Mr Broom, expecting rather more courtesy, said, 'I've got a proper handle to my name you know.' Back came the retort, 'Sorry! Hello Broomhandle!'

The First World War had finished by the time Tom was of an age to attend the Infants' class at the Portishead Council School, which was just across the road from Rhondda Villas. This was an elementary school, which educated children from infancy until they reached the school-leaving age of fourteen years. At eleven years old, some children would sit the Scholarship examination, and if they passed they would be eligible to attend one of the Bristol grammar schools. But this was not as straightforward a process as it sounds, for the parents of 'successful' children still had to contribute towards the cost of uniform, books, travel, daily food and, sometimes, a proportion of the school fees. The majority of parents could not afford such an outlay, or could not bring themselves to undergo the demeaning process of 'means-testing'. Many were afraid to let their children sit the examination in case they passed, so that quite often even the most worthy of pupils remained at their elementary schools until they were old enough to earn a little money towards their keep.

At Slade Road School, the education given was what would now be described as 'traditional'. Boys and girls sat in separate rows, were not allowed to turn round or to talk, and obeyed instantly the teacher's instructions on pain of physical retribution for any kind of indiscipline. Tom was a competent pupil at all times, but improved rapidly under the influence of Mr Churchley who looked after Standards V and VI. In October 1925, Tom was seventh out of ten in his age group, and in his report Mr Churchley mildly reprimanded him with the time-worn comment, 'Tom can do better than this.' It proved a sufficient spur and, in the following March just after his twelfth birthday, Tom came top of his group to merit the commendation, 'an excellent report'. From 1926 to 1928, in Standards VII and Ex. VII, Tom came under the Headmaster's supervision. Mr Barlow was generally pleased with Tom's progress: his attendance and punctuality were excellent, his conduct exemplary (presumably he was never caught), and his all-round results ranged from Good to Excellent. In view of Tom's later career, it is pleasing to note that his performance in Geography, Geometry and Mensuration[1] were consistently high.

On very cold days, when the children were released from their classes for morning playtime, Tom's mother would cross the road from Rhondda Villas to hand him a hot cup of cocoa through the railings! Mrs Broom was very much an old-fashioned mother (typical of her day) who, more often than not, would be found in the house caring for her home and family, which invariably headed her list of priorities. Louise Gough, a farmer's daughter, had been born at Hallen on the other side of the river Avon between Henbury and the Channel. As a young girl she obtained work as a maid 'in service' to a bank manager's family. When the family moved to live in the fashionable Woodhill, Louise moved with them, and that was how she came to meet John Broom and to marry him on 5 January 1911 at St Mary's Church, Henbury. Their life together was one of simple trust founded on love and decency, and those were the virtues that they nurtured in their children. On his twelfth birthday, Tom was urged by his mother always to be polite for, as she said, 'It costs nothing, and neither does telling the truth come to that.' The family attended St Peter's Church where Tom joined the choir. In the week before Christmas, they went round the village carol-singing, as well as further afield to the big houses in Woodhill and Woodland where some wealthy Bristol merchants lived. Whatever they collected paid for their annual visit to the pantomime at the Prince's Theatre on Park Row in Bristol (it and the ice-rink opposite were destroyed by German bombers in 1940–1941). Once, in 1925, the church choir made a special trip to London to visit the Wembley Exhibition.

In his spare time in the 1930s and 1940s, Mr Broom acted as an honorary caretaker of the British Legion hut. He prepared the room for meetings, generally tidying up and lighting the fire. In the summer he would trim the small lawn outside. However, Mr Broom's weekly luxury was to frequent the Working Men's Club to play solo whist with his friends, Frank Thomas (a horse and cab man), Boxer Brown (a bookie's runner) and Bill Acland (a local police constable). Often present as drinking companions were a member of the Butt family (of Clara Butt fame) and Tom Jay who, in days gone by, had been 'Charivari' in *Punch* magazine. It was not unknown for Mr Broom to mention his son's prowess on the rugby field. In the 1920s a relation of Sam Tucker (Bristol and England) had come to teach at the National School (St Peter's). 'Dear Old Pa', as he was known, organised schools' rugby in Portishead. It was a huge disappointment to Tom that when he was selected to play for Somerset in his last year at school, it was found that he was a few days too old to represent the County Under 14s XV.

When the time came for Tom to leave school, he was capable of earning his keep and of making his way in the world. He had been rigorously taught and properly brought up. His simple but worthy philosophy was, 'If you can't do someone a good turn, make sure you don't do him a bad one.' Almost at once, he was signed on at the Stoke Road Motor Garages and Engineering Works (situated where you can now find the Somerfield car park). Over the years, the place was known, also, as 'Coward and White', 'Spreag's' and 'Jenkins and Vickery'. Obtaining work in a garage was an exciting start to a young lad's career. Apart from the fact that the late 1920s and the following decade were years of depression with wholesale unemployment and poverty, so that finding any kind of work was a blessing, just being around cars was most satisfying for a fourteen-year-old boy. Owning cars in those days was an indication of real wealth so that very few cars were seen on local country roads. Indeed, little children living in cottages nearby would often flee to safety on hearing one spluttering towards them. Being involved with cars, engines and machines was to be at the forefront of the modern world. Tom was a kind of pioneer, and he had dreams of further excitements, but until he could realise them by joining the Royal Air Force, he made do with gaining the kind of experience that might be of benefit to him in the future.

Tom could take comfort from the fact that, at least, he could 'pilot' cars. Since most houses had not been designed with cars in mind, neither garages nor wide driveways had been provided, and since the streets were too narrow to have cars parked on them, several vehicles were stored at the Stoke Road garage. Tom was required, as part of his work, to move them from one spot to another in the yard. Within three years of leaving school, Tom obtained his own driving licence, and then was often instructed to deliver cars to their owners' homes, possibly as far away as the distant Woodlands or Nore Road. Sometimes he was tipped a shilling (5p), a useful sum for it was more than the cost of a gallon of petrol.

An additional experience for Tom was using a telephone. Owning one was regarded as a sign of affluence; there were not many residences in the village that could boast one. However, the garage owner, Mr Spreag, could be contacted at Portishead 145. There was no need for eleven-digit numbers as there was no countrywide dialling system then. If you were outside the immediate area, your call would have to be routed through various telephone exchanges. Using the telephone was quite a rare event and, for some people, a stressful process to be wary of.

Of course, what was of even greater significance to Tom was that he was now in receipt of 12s 6d a week (12 shillings and 6 pence or 62½p), of which he gave his mother 10 shillings (50p) towards his keep, a modest but crucial contribution to the family budget that Tom was both proud and happy to make.

Tom intended to apply for RAF entrance as soon as he reached his eighteenth birthday. This would be in January 1932. Well before then he started to sort things out. In March 1931 he asked Mr Coward, the Works Manager and a Chartered Mechanical Engineer, if he would provide a reference. His report was quite flattering for he described Tom as an industrious worker, eager to learn, an excellent timekeeper, a capable and cautious driver, and a very civil and strictly honest lad. When it was time to make his application, he required two further references. Mr Spreag and Dr Charles

Wigan, a distinguished medical man and the father of Eve Wigan, Portishead's noted historian, agreed to write on his behalf. The former had no hesitation in recommending Tom as 'a suitable candidate for engagement in that branch of His Majesty's forces in which he desires to serve.' Dr Wigan declared that he had known Tom since birth and had always found him suitable for any post requiring intelligence, sobriety and courage. No doubt these glowing testimonials were thoroughly deserved, but little did two of them know that in the distant future Tom would not best be remembered for his caution or his abstention.

The family had known for a long time of Tom's keenness to enlist and, though his mother may have had reservations and many a secret fear, his decision was approved, though regretted, by his father, his older sister, Muriel, and his younger brothers, Bob and Peter. His friends, of course, were rather envious of his daring in leaving dear old Posset for the great unknown. And so, assuming that he would be found fit at the medical examination to be held at Bristol, Tom would now enter a new phase of his life, away from the safety of familiar haunts and the comfort of village friendships.

CHAPTER TWO

Initiation

Once Tom's application had been processed, he was ordered to report to London for tests, both mental and physical. So it was that on 3 May 1932 (a date imprinted on his memory), he was given a lift on the pillion of Fred Small's motorbike to catch the 5 a.m. train from Temple Meads station in Bristol. Only once before had Tom been to London, and then as one of a supervised group, so that this train journey, as well as being a kind of glorious adventure, had elements of stress in it. He reached Gwyder House, an Air Ministry building in Whitehall, safely and was duly assessed. Of the eighteen young men who attended, only three passed the written and medical examinations, and they were driven immediately to the recruitment centre at West Drayton. There, Tom enlisted for 'nine and three', that is, nine years in the Service and three with the Reserve. After attesting that he would serve his King and Country faithfully, a sixpenny telegram (date stamped 3 May 1932) was sent home with the succinct message:

PASSED – EVERYTHING O.K. – RECRUIT BROOM

West Drayton was just a sorting centre, so after a couple of days the new recruits were transferred to the RAF station at Uxbridge (on the north-west fringe of London) where they were to receive their basic training.

It was at Uxbridge that Tom learned that whereas you might join the Navy to see the world, you became an airman to scrub it. It seemed as if his waking hours were spent entirely on fatigues whilst waiting for enough recruits to gather to form a squad of thirty airmen. 'Fatigues' meant performing lowly drudgeries like potato-peeling, litter-picking, floor-scrubbing and white-washing, tasks that fully trained airmen were not expected to carry out. It was most frustrating for an enthusiastic volunteer to wait throughout May,

June and July for more men to enlist. He wrote an optimistic letter home at the end of May in which he reported, 'I am still enjoying myself and putting on weight and am getting taller. I expect you will see the difference in August.' He mentioned, also, that he had seen Helen Hayes in 'Lullaby' and that he was looking forward to 'Frankenstein' being featured in the local cinema. He did add a slightly glum comment, 'We are still Room Orderlies.' Little did he dream that another two months of fatigues lay ahead. Even when the three months' basic training eventually started, as well as parade-ground drilling, fitness-training in the gymnasium, and learning the use of firearms, the recruits had to perform a vast amount of 'spit and polish' to make sure that belts, buttons and boots were spotlessly clean. Yet, surprisingly, Tom rather enjoyed the process of being moulded into the kind of shape that would help to qualify him as an airman. Through suffering the chores together, a fine comradeship was being developed that gave the squad a group pride. This was demonstrated when they lined up to cheer Sergeant Ferris as he ran the marathon from Windsor to London, an event that he won for the seventh time in eight years.

There were several gifted athletes who used the track facilities at Uxbridge. Three of them were preparing for the Olympic Games to be held at Los Angeles that very year, G. Rampling (of the Army) in the 440 yards, D.O. Finlay (43 Squadron) in the 120 yards' hurdles and R.H. Thomas (40 Squadron) in the mile. Those recruits who were reasonably athletic acted as pacers around the cinder track. They were spaced at intervals and were expected at the appropriate moment to burst away for a few dozen yards to be a spur to the serious runners. However, despite the pride that they felt in being involved, most recruits regarded it as wise policy not to shine in the various games and sports, for there was always the chance that success would keep them at Uxbridge for years, possibly to the detriment of their longed-for RAF careers. It was rumoured that one gifted half-miler was retained as a storeman at the station for many a long day despite wishing to leave. Another lesson very quickly learnt was to claim membership of a religious group other than the Church of England. All Anglicans had to attend a compulsory church parade on Sunday mornings. Catholics, Jews and Odds and Sods (Methodists, Baptists, Presbyterians and others) were instructed to fall out and return to their billets for private worship.

On most free Saturdays, Tom and his friends went to see one football match or another. He remembers in particular a visit to Highbury to see Arsenal (in the days of Herbert Chapman's all-conquering pre-war side) play Everton, the team that Tom supported. The visitors won, the only goal being scored by Dixie Dean[2] with a header. In contrast to today's boorishness, it was perfectly safe for Tom to cheer Everton whilst standing in the middle of a group of Arsenal supporters.

After the passing-out parade at the end of October, the squad was kept on station at Uxbridge. Its smart efficiency was required for the Lord Mayor's Show. Altogether, about a hundred airmen marched proudly through the streets of the capital to the accompaniment of the Central Band of the RAF. Very soon after this, the squad, with others, provided a Guard of Honour on Armistice Day at the Cenotaph Memorial Ceremony in the presence of the King. What an experience for a young Posset lad within six months of leaving his village. Following this, Tom spent his three days' leave with his aunt, whose husband worked on Lord Carnarvon's estate at Highclere near Newbury. In the same month, November 1932, Tom left Uxbridge, though he was destined to return many years later to dine in the Officers' Mess, which, in the past few months, he had scrubbed clean so many times.

Tom was posted to 40(Bomber) Squadron stationed at RAF Abingdon as an AC2 – the lowest proper rank in the Air Force. The squadron had been formed the previous year and was commanded by S/Ldr Malcolm Taylor. 40(B) Squadron was the first to be equipped with Fairey Gordon two-seater bombers. The first overseas squadron to have them was 6(B) Squadron in the Middle East, which Tom would join later. The Fairey was a lumbering aircraft powered by a single 525-hp engine. It had a maximum speed of 145 mph and a range of 600 miles with a 500-pound bomb load carried under the wings. It was armed with two .303 in. machine-guns, one Vickers gun forward-firing and the other Lewis gun firing aft.

However, Tom spent his first few weeks in the cookhouse! As he was a driving-licence holder (they were few and far between), he was invited to take a driver's course. Tom declined the offer because he had been informed that an RAF driver was classified in the lowest pay group (Group 5). He had been well advised, also, to 'get a trade', and very soon he obtained a transfer to the Armoury to learn about guns, bullets and bombs. He enjoyed the experience for now he could claim that his work had something to do with aeroplanes.

Unlike the Army, where a soldier generally stayed with the same people in the same Regiment throughout his military service, in the RAF there were two-year postings, so that a tour of duty at one station would be followed by another tour in a different station. In this way, there were squadron changes all the time. Tom knew that he would be at Abingdon for a fixed period only, so he decided to use his time profitably by taking advantage of the educational facilities there, a surprisingly mature attitude in a teenager who had left school nearly five years earlier. His decision was to stand him in good stead in later years.

Nevertheless, it was not all work at Abingdon, and Tom continued to take a full part in the sporting side of service life. As previously mentioned, one of his heroes at RAF Abingdon was Sergeant Thomas, the champion miler who had taken part in the Olympics at Los Angeles. Tom himself was more attracted to team games, and he played regularly for the station rugby team as a wing-forward (or flanker as it is now known). Usually, on Wednesdays, he was just one of three other-rankers amongst a dozen or so officers, but on Saturdays the teams consisted entirely of other-rankers.

On Wednesday afternoons, Oxford University colleges would often provide the opposition. The airmen looked forward to playing away for, as soon as the match ended, fifteen pints of shandy awaited them before they left to tuck-in to tea and crumpets back at the college. Sometimes, the refreshments would be presented on valuable silver salvers. Another fixture that Tom remembers well was the match against the Sixth Formers of Radley College (coached by Guy Morgan, a Welsh international). It was an interesting experience for a country village lad to mix with the sons of gentry in the school's Great Hall but, of course, it was not in Tom's nature to take advantage of his happier upbringing! On those Wednesdays when there was no rugby, he would willingly don a goalkeeper's jersey to play for any XI that happened to be short of players. In fact, Tom played regularly for the station soccer team until the rugby season started, and played soccer again when the rugby was over.

There was not enough money available for much gallivanting, but on most Friday nights Tom would go with his friend to the 'Beehive' in Abingdon. 'Skats', an AC2 like Tom, was a talented pianist who would entertain the customers by playing the latest popular songs. Sitting next to 'Skats' by the piano, Tom benefited greatly from the free beer that flowed throughout the night in appreciation of his friend's accomplishment. Perhaps it was at the 'Beehive' that Tom developed his life-long dedication to real ale.

On one occasion, he was checked for his alcohol content. Another friend of Tom's, AC2 Crosby, had crashed his motorcycle when returning from his leave in West Hartlepool. As a kindness, Tom picked up the bike and looked after it. Since he had been given permission to use it, one evening he took another friend, AC1 Tingley, on the pillion and rode into Abingdon. Unfortunately, just after leaving camp, the bike slid on a patch of gravel and Tom was thrown over the handlebar. He suffered a badly grazed face, the faint scars of which may still be seen on his nose and chin to this day. He spent three days in the RAF sick-bay and was examined by a doctor who suspected that Tom had been drinking. The usual quick tests of the moving finger in front of the eyes and of walking a straight line showed that Tom was innocent of blame. This was just as well, for if he had been found to be suffering from 'self-inflicted injuries', he would have been charged 1s 6d for each day spent in care, a significant amount when taken out of a weekly wage of 12s 6d.

Being stationed at RAF Abingdon was an attractive posting because of its relative proximity to Portishead, just 70 miles away as the crow flies. However, it took a good part of a day's travelling when Tom took his leave, The train journey was split into four separate runs, Abingdon to Culham, Culham to Didcot, Didcot to Bristol and Bristol to Portishead.

During his second year at Abingdon, Tom applied and was accepted for a six-month Armourer's course at Eastchurch on the Isle of Sheppey in the Thames estuary. Of course, this was further away from home, but Tom felt that it was essential for him to make positive moves to further his service career. So, from April until October 1935, he was back at school once more and, though it was an uncomfortable experience, he thrived and came fifth out of fifty students. He was promoted to AC1 (Aircraftman First Class) and, in addition, he was now a fully qualified armourer. Tom's only regret was that if he had gained a result only 1.2 per cent better, he would have been promoted to LAC (Leading Aircraftman). During his stay at Eastchurch, Tom kept up his interest in rugby and played regularly for the station team. He also played soccer for the side representing the Armourers and, memorably, took part in one match against Gillingham Reserves at left-half (a wing-back in modern parlance).

From Eastchurch, Tom was posted to Upavon, near Devizes in Wiltshire. The Central Flying School was based on Salisbury Plain, and from it hardly anything of interest could be seen except for RAF Netheravon, which was about 6 miles distant. Whereas Tom had been delighted with his previous postings, he was not enamoured of Upavon as there was very little to keep him busy. Though he was the only armourer there, his services were not really needed, for the aircraft on station were for flying training only. It was at Upavon that all RAF Flying Instructors were trained, and where pilots learned the skills of flying aeroplanes to their limits, for example, experiencing and correcting downward spins.

To Tom's relief, his stay was brief. Very soon, on the Daily Routine Orders board, he read a notice of preliminary warning that he was to be posted overseas. Though it is a silly comment to make about an airman, Tom was an 'old soldier' by now and quite ready for the wider world. He was expecting to serve abroad for five years, two of them in a 'hot' station and a further three years in either India or Egypt. So it was that on a Sunday evening in January 1936, he wrote home to wish his family well and to express the hope that the years would roll by quickly so that he would see them all again very soon.

CHAPTER THREE

Guarding the Empire

In January 1936, Tom boarded HM Troopship *Dilwara* at Southampton, and sailed from there the day before the funeral of His Majesty King George V, part of whose Empire Tom was now going to defend. For ten days the ship steamed through the Bay of Biscay, past Gibraltar and Malta to Port Said in Egypt at the far end of the Mediterranean Sea, and from there through the Suez Canal and the Red Sea to Port Sudan. At Port Sudan, sixty airmen disembarked bound for Khartoum, the capital of the Sudan, to join 47(Bomber) Squadron and become part of the Sudan Defence Force. Ahead of them lay a twenty-four-hour hot and dusty train journey.

The Sudan Defence Force was responsible for the whole country, an area more than twelve times larger than the whole of Britain. The force consisted of two Army battalions and 47(B) Squadron. Tom's particular duty was to arm the aircraft of 'A' Flight. These were Fairey Gordons, which were soon to be replaced with Vickers Vincents. The Vincent, a three-seater bomber, was powered by a Bristol Pegasus 660-hp engine, but the only advantage it had over the Gordon was that it could carry a bomb load of 1100 pounds.

The Gordons were modified as float-planes for use on the River Nile and other waters during the rainy season, when the aircraft became the only means of reaching some District Commissioners in the more outlandish spots of the Empire in Africa[3].

A British soldier or airman could be sent to serve in any one of these outposts of Empire. Tours abroad normally lasted five years, but the length of service in any one place depended largely on the climatic conditions prevailing or on the seriousness of any local conflicts that might occur. Certainly, the Sudan was recognised as a 'hot' posting, and a maximum of two years would be spent there.

Though the British tend to look back to the days of the Empire with some longing and much pride, the people who were forcibly colonised do not have a similarly rose-coloured view of that era, for the English, no matter where they went, insisted that their characteristics, both of custom and language, should have precedence over whatever indigenous cultures existed. There is no doubt that the natives were treated as members of an under-class – as 'natives' in the most primitive sense. However, the one great benefit that no one would dispute is the existence of today's Commonwealth of Nations.

The British Empire before the Second World War

1. Canada and Newfoundland
2. West Indies – British Honduras, British Guiana, Bermuda, Bahamas, Turks and Caicos, Jamaica, Virgin Islands, Anguilla, St Kitts and Nevis, Antigua and Barbuda, Montserrat, Dominica, St Lucia, Barbados, St Vincent, Grenada, Trinidad and Tobago
3. Falklands, Graham Land, South Georgia, Sandwich Islands, Atlantic Islands (Tristan da Cunha, St Helena, Ascension)
4. Mediterranean – Gibraltar, Malta, Cyprus
5. West Africa – Nigeria, Gold Coast, Gambia, Sierra Leone, Cameroons, Togo
6. Middle East – Palestine, Iraq, Transjordan, Kuwait, Bahrain, Qatar, Muscat and Oman, Trucial States, Aden
7. Africa – Egypt (Suez), Sudan, Somaliland, Uganda, Kenya, Tanganyika, N. Rhodesia, Nyasaland, S. Rhodesia, South Africa, Bechuanaland, Basutoland, Swaziland, South West Africa
8. India (inc. Pakistan and Bangladesh), Ceylon, Burma, Indian Ocean islands (Maldives, Seychelles, Mauritius)
9. Far East – Hong Kong, Malaya, Singapore, North Borneo, Sarawak, Brunei, Papua New Guinea, Solomon Islands, trading stations on Sumatra
10. Australia, New Zealand, Fiji, Tonga, Western Samoa, the Pacific islands (e.g. New Hebrides, Gilbert, Ellice, Cook, Santa Cruz, Phoenix)

The 47(B) Squadron and Tom's 'A' Flight were kept quite busy. Civilian as well as military VIPs were flown to wherever they were required in the Sudan. Even the Bishop of Egypt and Sudan was taken round parts of his diocese. The airmen felt quite safe with him on board! The country's borders had to be guarded: movement across them was discouraged, especially of cattle-rustlers and slave-traders. During 1936 there was considerable tension because of the Italian–Abyssinian war that was taking place nearby. If the League of Nations had acted positively to thwart the Italian aggression, the British forces in the Sudan, quite possibly, could have been the first military group involved. Wing Commander Ritchie wisely placed emphasis on readiness for action. Much time was spent on bombing practice (with dummy bombs only), but front and rear gunners were allowed to use live rounds of ammunition, presumably because bullets were much cheaper than bombs. There were frequent short reconnaissance flights towards the borders when numerous essential exercises were carried out. For example, upper-air temperatures were recorded at a height of 15,000 feet, and photography tasks, including air-to-air camera-gun work, had to be completed as well.

Meanwhile, in Portishead, Tom was much missed by his family. His mother kept all his letters and, no doubt, read them over and over again to keep her eldest son close to her. From the very first week that he spent in the Sudan, Tom's letters provided a diary of events that were happening a few thousand miles away – from the ends of the earth as it seemed seventy years ago.

In abridged note form, his letters read:

14.2.36: Arrived Tuesday about 5.15 p.m. after travelling for 24 hours from Port Sudan. Went over miles and miles of desert. Quartered in marquees: no room in the bungalows until the men we're replacing have moved on to their new station. On the banks of the Blue Nile the weather is glorious with temperatures around 95 degrees F in the shade. (This after leaving England in the middle of winter!) Topees must be worn from dawn to dusk. Airmail is expensive if anything bulky is sent, so send copies of Evening World by sea for 2d (app. ½p) not by air for 2s 6d (12½p). Saw lots of BP petrol tankers in Port Said harbour. Have seen hundreds of goats, donkeys and camels. Camel caravans often pass the gates. Ivory is cheap (and silk dresses) but can't send any home as customs duty is expensive. Went to open-air cinema in Khartoum and saw Gaumont News of the King's funeral procession.

29.2.36: [Leap Year's Day. Any man born on that day would have celebrated his nineteenth birthday in the year 2006 – a teenager in his seventieth year!] 103 degrees F but fairly cool in the bungalows. We shall wish farewell to the old draft with a 5-course dinner. The chickens came by lorry today. Selected to play rugby and football for the station against army teams. Surprised how far natives can kick football in bare feet. Visited Omdurman[4], the largest native town in the world – we had to go in groups of four with one of us armed. Water melon plantations on banks of Nile. Locusts like giant grasshoppers 4 inches long. Lizards are harmless, but not the scorpions and the tarantula spiders. Listened to Henry Hall on the wireless playing 'Sugar Plum'. Ask Peter to keep me up-to-date with the latest songs. In reply to his query, the 2½ on the stamp means 2½ piastres (6d). There are 5 piastres in a shilling and 100 in a £1 note. (N.B. a decimal currency as we have now in the UK)

28.3.36: Watch has packed up – too much sand for it. Tell Stan Slocombe a 3d stamp will do. Have written to Tom Berg. Now that Peter starts work at Wills there will be a little bit extra for you. I pass on the Evening World to a chap from Trowbridge, Rose by name, whose brother plays for Bristol Rovers Reserves. Expect to go to Alexandria on leave in June or July.

18.4.36: On Good Friday went to the zoo. On Saturday went on picnic to Gebel Aulia. River too low for paddle-steamer. Dam being built at cost of £2,500,000 to store Nile flood water at a high level all year round, instead of being flooded for a few months and then very low for rest of year. It will irrigate the land for 180 miles downstream. 5000 natives working on the dam. Crops will be grown throughout year. Caught tarantula in room – body 3 inches and legs 3 inches. Have seen snakes, mongooses, vultures and hawks. One chap stung by scorpion had to spend couple of days in hospital. A few miles down country there are elephants, lions and rhinos. Roads in Khartoum are lined with trees, with palm trees on the river bank. Went to pictures on Monday evening. Due soon, Harold Lloyd in 'Milky Way'. Strange to see native women working as street *sweepers. Wives have to carry heavy loads for their husbands! Native women are covered from head to foot. They wear veils so that only their eyes can be seen.*

15.5.36: Fierce sandstorm followed by torrential rain. Has to be seen to be believed. Could see wall of sand 3000 feet high coming towards us.[5] Interruptions to mail as Imperial Airways delayed by crashes. Mr H.L. Brook landed on a trip to the Cape in a monoplane powered by a 40-hp two-cylinder engine! Mrs Mollison[6] welcomed when she landed during her flight from the Cape on the way home to England.

30.5.36: Letter arrived last night – had to pay 24 milliems (5½d) surcharge as it was overweight. Look forward to receiving your letters every Friday. It's the highlight of the week. Gimblett's doing well – should be picked for England. [The Somerset opener was selected to play against India in the first two tests.] Visited by a Daily Telegraph reporter and we put on a show for him. Looks as if the unemployment problem in Portishead is being solved. [Rearmament was beginning to take place. As well as the Services being enlarged, there was more work available at the Bristol Aeroplane Company where the production of Blenheim bombers was being speeded up.]

13.6.36: There are people suffering from sunstroke – they haven't been wearing topees. Rains due soon and the Sudanese are digging trenches to carry water away. Powerful moonlight – can almost read by it. Couple of weeks ago, had a 'flip' in a seaplane – apart from landing on water, no difference. Already looking forward to October when new draft comes in and we shall be the seniors. We'll welcome them with a party – any excuse for a good time. Good selection of pictures – 'Roberta', 'Desire' and many others.

In August 1936 Tom went on a fortnight's leave to Egypt with fourteen other airmen. Even by plane it was a long trip, for the aircraft used, the Vickers Valentia, was a troop-carrier that could only cruise at 80 mph. It had a crew of five, including two pilots in an open cockpit, and it could carry up to twenty-two passengers. Valentias from 216 (BT) Squadron were based at Heliopolis, near Cairo, and were used to train new pilots as well. Valentias and Gordons were still flying from RAF Habbaniyah in Iraq as late as 1941. From Khartoum to Wadi Halfa took 5½ hours. After refuelling there, it took another 3½ hours to reach Luxor where they made an overnight stop. From Luxor to Heliopolis took over 3½ hours and from there to Aboukir another 1½ hours. So it took the best part of two days to fly from Khartoum to Egypt.

22.8.36: Left at 6 a.m. on August Bank Holiday Monday and arrived at Luxor at 4 p.m. – stopped for petrol twice – at Atbara and Wadi Halfa. Spent the night at Luxor and saw the remains of Tutankhamen's tomb. Left at 8 a.m. – landed at Assuit at midday to refill – arrived at Aboukir about 4 p.m. very tired. Flew over desert most of the way. Lovely weather in Egypt, the beach sandy, water blue and warm – raft anchored some way out to sea. In evening went to Alexandria – surprised how modern it looks, just like an English city with museums (remains from the tombs), picture houses, hotels, a casino and cabarets. Every nationality under the sun in the streets of Alexandria. Fleet has left the harbour – no battleships now. Stayed at Air Force camp, but not under usual discipline. Saw some old remains at Aboukir – went into various caves and passages.

5.9.36: Mail delayed 2 days because of rain. Nile in flood. As it overflows at about the same time every year no one is caught napping on the river bank! Writing this at 5 p.m. having just woken from a nap. Papers from home more interesting now that the football season has started. Doing quite well for Station 1st XI against army teams and occasionally a native side. May have to fly to Gebeit just north of Port Sudan (about 400 miles away). Considering the reputation of this part of the world I am keeping really well. Will have a shower, a spot of dinner, then shop for some shirts in Khartoum. Hope we win back the Ashes and that Barnett and Hammond do well. A pity that Gimblett was left out. [England won the first two tests, then lost the other three – the first time ever for this to happen! Barnett scored one century and Hammond a double century.]

26.9.36: Heatwave continues, but only 106 degrees F now. Another sandstorm followed by torrential rain yesterday – should be the last of the year. Glad to hear you have a new St John ambulance. Air race to Johannesburg should pass over here 9 o'clock onwards on Tuesday evening – flares to be placed on runway in case of emergency.

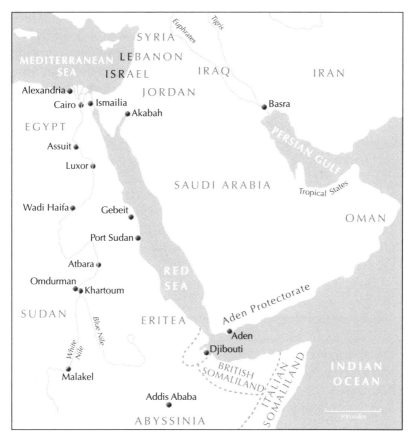

3.10.36: *Sir Phillip Sassoon (Under Secretary of State for Air) pleased with Inspection and Guard of Honour. His Imperial Airways plane was stuck at Malakel with a broken undercarriage – 450 miles south of Khartoum – with only a bug-ridden rest house. Aircraft sent to rescue him. On his return, he spent the evening with us in the canteen and he paid for all the beer until the bar closed. He's a most popular visitor in Khartoum. Had a good view of the air-race. We were allowed on to the drome. Usually dark here by 6.30. The first one got here at 1.40 a.m. on Wednesday. Captain Halse was followed by a few others over the next day or two. Khartoum is also a night stop for Imperial Airways. The Accounts section ran a book. I backed Halse but he crashed 600 miles from the finish. Scott[7] won at odds of 6 to 1.*

10.10.36: *Mr C.W.A. Scott landed here this morning on his way back. There will be four airliners calling here after today – 2 of the Hannibal type and two de Havilland 86s. We have beaten both Army battalions and that's not bad for they have 1000 men and we've only 120. Expecting to see 'Mutiny on the Bounty' soon. Two or three of our footballers suffering from cartilage trouble, including one who played centre-half for England some years ago.*

17.10.36: Boat fever running high – new draft should be leaving England next week – reception committee to organise a welcome party with guard of honour in fancy dress banging tin drums. Christmas won't be long – prizes given for best decorated billet – ours will be dressed to resemble a garden fete with sideshows – The Bearded Lady, Ringing The Bull, Revolving Horse, Staking A Claim, Darts, Roulette, Fortune Telling, etc. with all of us kitted out like village people – the parson and policeman – or as cartoon characters like Popeye. Next week we've got four league games.

24.10.36: Want nothing for Christmas, just a nice long letter, though a cake would be wonderful. The draft leaves England today – in the canteen tonight we shall be singing 'For those in peril on the sea'. The cricket team is due to play the Khartoum Club in a two-day match. We're still leading in the football league. All the grass that appeared in the rainy season has now disappeared. A chance next week to go shooting. [For a young man keen on team games, there could hardly have been a better posting than Khartoum. As well as a charity match that evening, Tom was expecting to play cricket over the weekend, followed by two games of rugby and a football match in the week.]

2.1.37: Had wonderful time at Christmas with sunshine and blue skies. Thinking of you in cold England. On the lawn we had a miniature golf course. Some billets were dressed as Wild West saloons (with cowboys and Indians), or as old English Inns with horses borrowed and dressed as if ready for the hunt, and with snow (salt) scattered about. Some billets were decorated as if they were pantomime scenes. At dinner we were waited on by the officers. The party atmosphere lasted for most of the week with several Treasure Hunts and games of Polo with borrowed donkeys and hockey sticks. Playing full-back tonight in rugby match. I was vaccinated last Wednesday. Mum – your two cakes took some beating. We had saved up a shilling a week for some time to pay for the parties at Christmas.

19.1.37: 'A' Flight with four aircraft took part in co-operation exercises with the Sudan Defence Force and, as Armourer, I had to go. We went some 400 miles south-west from the base to a small native village where there were just two Britishers, the District Commissioner and his Assistant. The landing ground was a clearing in the forest. The area was then fenced off and ringed with fire at night to keep out wild animals. Lots of Jebels (big hills between 1000 and 2000 feet high – rocks formed by volcanic eruption). Time to spare so went shooting, guinea fowl mainly, but jackals, hyenas, wild pig, and gazelle as well. [In fact, Tom twice escaped danger when a scorpion crawled across the back of his hand and when a tarantula lodged in his shirt pocket.] Went through the jungle in a Ford V8. Saw many native tribes, all carrying spears and completely naked. Returned to base to give air displays for sheiks.[8]

Tom's final Khartoum letters to his mother described some eventful few months. In July, he reported that he had been on a boat trip on the Blue Nile, and that a new flying-boat service enabled them to receive mail on three days a week. He regretted that he would not be able to have home leave as he had to serve a year in Egypt, but he was glad to say that in a written test he had come top of the Armament Section with 82 per cent. In August, as well as mentioning Amelia Earhart's visit[9], he recorded that a German plane had been lost some 700 miles away in the Sudd, a swamp of impenetrable papyrus stems and tall grasses covering a huge area in southern Sudan near the Kenyan border. As it would have taken at least a week to reach the isolated crew overland, parachute drops of food, water and serum for snake bites were made daily until the crew was rescued by boat.

In 1937, also, one of the pilots employed to fly an Empire flying-boat (*Cassiopeia*) from the harbour at Alexandria to Southampton was a Don Bennett of Imperial Airways. He was also the pilot who did the original test proving-flight from England to Cape Town. He landed at Wadi Halfa and Khartoum. Some years later he would play an important role in Tom's life.

25.9.37: Am counting the days (56) when the relief is due to arrive. We lost the last match 157 – 118. Seamer got 82. (He and Mitchell-Innes, also of Oxford University and Somerset and stationed at Khartoum, have entries in Wisden.) Captained a scratch side last

week against a combined XI of RAMC, RASC, RAOC and RA units.
We got them out for 21 and 46. We made 163 for 5 declared. I
opened and got 25 including a 6 and a 4. Thanks for the papers,
which are eagerly awaited for the football results. The Nile is flooded
again.

Tom's service in Khartoum came to an end in November 1937. It
was time for half the establishment to depart for new duties
elsewhere. Tom was destined for 6(B) Squadron at Ismailia, one of
the RAF stations that guarded the Suez Canal. Though glad to be
leaving, Tom had thoroughly enjoyed his two years at Khartoum.
His new posting involved a return train journey to Port Sudan and,
most appropriately for Tom, a trip along the Red Sea to Port Tewfiq
on HM Troopship *Somersetshire*.

At this time, towards the end of 1937, the Arab–Jewish conflict
was raging. 'C' Flight in Palestine needed to be strengthened, so Tom
and others were detached from the Squadron to serve there. Just
before Christmas, and travelling in daylight (night travel was too
dangerous during the troubles), they reached the RAF station at
Ramleh. In his letter home, Tom described how pleasant the
countryside was with its greenery, and orange and almond groves.
He mentioned that bags of oranges were placed in the dining hall
every day. He commented as well how much more comfortable it
was at night compared with Khartoum with temperatures about 15
degrees lower. Of course, he sent his best wishes for Christmas and
said that he hoped he would be home to celebrate the next one. He
added that, though he missed his family and friends, the two years
he had spent overseas had done him a world of good. It had
broadened his mind and given him a different outlook on life. He
was quite glad that he had not stayed in Portishead and missed
seeing anything of the world. A young man needed such
experiences, and to emphasise his point he said that he was looking
forward to visiting Bethlehem at Christmas.

At Ramleh, S/Ldr Hobson had under his command four Hawker
Harts, possibly the finest aircraft of its day. Two pilots were on
stand-by duty at all times awaiting emergency calls from the Army
patrols. Every morning, Tom had to rearm the aircraft with 20-
pound bombs. The front Vickers machine-gun, which fired through
the propellers, had to be loaded with 400 rounds of ammunition.

Also, Tom had to secure the mounting of the air-gunner's Lewis gun. On the sounding of a klaxon (a wailing, urgent siren) everybody rushed into action. The Hawker Harts' engines were periodically fired to maintain the correct oil temperature necessary for a prompt start. Thus, they were at all times in a state of readiness. When called for assistance, two aircraft would leave immediately and, if wireless messages were received asking for further help, the other two would take off. When there were prolonged engagements, Tom had a further duty of restocking the Bomb Store.

Because of the worsening situation in Palestine, with the Arabs in revolt at Jewish immigration and land-purchase, and the Jews agitating for greater independence, the rest of 6(B) Squadron arrived at Ramleh, and 'C' Flight was relieved of duties – at Ramleh, that is. It was about this time that the Army and the Air Force were criticised for using air bombardment against tribesmen and their families in a way that was 'unworthy of a civilised nation'. It was almost as if the Hawker Hart had been given the task of policing that part of the Empire. Aircrew, who were always in danger of being shot down by tribesmen in Transjordan and Iraq, were given what were coarsely known as 'goolie chits'. These slips of paper offered substantial rewards for airmen rescued unharmed.

'C' Flight was transferred to Semakh in the Jordan valley, on the banks of the Sea of Galilee where the Jordan ran out on its path towards the Dead Sea. It was difficult to believe that this spot was 900 feet below sea level. There were just three huts, one for officers, one for other ranks, and one that they shared as a cookhouse and mess-hall. The fifteen of them seemed to live on goat's meat and any fish they might catch in the lake. The camp was surrounded by a very high barbed-wire fence. Nearby, the Transjordan Frontier Force was encamped. At night, their searchlight swept the three huts and the parked planes. There was no aerodrome as such, but on receipt of an emergency call, the gates would be swung open and the planes would take off. Most of the flying operations were conducted in support of the Frontier Force, on reconnaissance missions usually, but sometimes the planes were ordered up just to demonstrate that the RAF was always ready for action. There were occasions when the Flight had to attack ground targets with machine-guns and bombs.

Despite the constant tension, life at Semakh was very pleasant. It was made rather more interesting when Air Commodore Harris, the Air Officer Commanding in Palestine and Transjordan, paid a visit. In later years, of course, he was to achieve great fame as 'Bomber' Harris. The Army Commander in Palestine at that time, General Wavell, became equally renowned. However, the daily routine was a little more mundane. Before breakfast, they refreshed themselves with a swim in the lake, but the remainder of the day was spent on stand-by duty. One of the airmen was a carpenter-rigger and, with some help, he built a two-man canoe that provided the men with much fun on the lake. When they were stood down and were free to leave camp, they would go to Tiberias for a meal and a few drinks. There seemed to be a very good reason for having small infusions of alcohol regularly, for they had noticed during their service in a hot climate that the people who suffered from dysentery were more often than not teetotallers!

In Transjordan and Iraq (at one time, part of the Ottoman Empire) the presence of the RAF dissuaded the Turks from attempting to reoccupy the land. (Though Iraq had been independent since 1932, an RAF presence remained at Habbaniyah during the war, with as many as five squadrons on base.) Now, however, the RAF's major responsibility was to keep open the oil pipe-line that ran from Iraq to Haifa in Palestine. As it was above ground, it was an easy target for rebelling tribesmen. Brushwood would be piled up beneath and around the pipe and set on fire. When the pipe was very hot, rifle fire would pierce it resulting in a most spectacular blaze. The Squadron saw plenty of action and, for a 'peace-time' unit, earned a record number of gallantry awards. Though not directly involved in operations, even an armourer's work could be dangerous, for after Tom had left, his replacement and two others were killed when unloading bombs from a returning plane.

In Europe at this time, the dictators of Spain, Italy and Germany were rearming. As part of Britain's response to the perceived danger, it became necessary for the RAF to be equipped with newer, faster aircraft. Gunners (at 1s 6d a day or 7½p) acting as part-time observers no longer fulfilled requirements. When Tom read a notice on Daily Routine Orders that tradesmen in Groups 1 and 2 could apply for retraining as Air Observers, he sensed an opportunity to make his boyhood dream of flying with the RAF a reality. Tom applied and, after a series of medical examinations and interviews with various Commanders (Station, Palestine and Transjordan, and Middle East) he was accepted. The successful applicants serving in the Middle East were instructed to report for embarkation at Port Said, but when they reached there they found that there was no troopship available, so they had to make do with the Orient Line's steamship *Orontes*.

They travelled as civilians, but the crew knew who they were and thoroughly spoiled them. The liner called at Naples, Toulon, Gibraltar and Plymouth before docking at Tilbury at the end of August 1938. So came to an end another phase of Tom's career in the RAF.

CHAPTER 4

A Dream Come True

Tom started his Air Observer's course in October 1938 at the Air Navigation School at Leconfield in Yorkshire. Back at school once more for three months, he had to learn the intricacies of Navigation and Photography. The aircraft in which he trained were Handley Page Heyfords, lumbering biplanes with huge, unretractable spats covering the wheels.

With various pilots, Tom did about twenty hours' flying in October alone. Most cross-country flights lasted for 1½ hours and involved map-reading, course-plotting and photography. Other flights lasted longer, when Tom's ability to cope with frequent alterations of course was tested. On New Year's Day 1939, Tom and his fellow trainees were in Belfast on their way to Aldergrove for the Bombing and Gunnery part of the course. For six weeks, Lough Neagh was used for live air-firing and bombing practice. On his return to Leconfield, Tom was promoted to Sergeant and, of course, he could now wear proudly his Observer's badge.

In February, Tom was posted to 105(B) Squadron at RAF Harwell in Berkshire to gain experience in Fairey Battles. On 23 February, he had his first flight as a qualified Air Observer when he plotted a course to Brighton and back for his pilot, Flying Officer Wheatley. This was supposed to be a simple test before he was assigned to a pilot of his own, Sergeant Costello-Bowen. With LAC Hughes they formed a crew that, a few days later, flew together for the first time on an altitude test at a height of 22,000 feet. In March, Tom flew with several different pilots including a Pilot Officer Lascelles (presumably of the Harewood family) who, when they were close to the ancestral estate, asked Tom to change course so that he could 'shoot up' the stately home.

Throughout the spring and early-summer months of 1939, the Squadron was extremely busy. As well as flying across country to practise bombing Peterborough (simulation bombing, of course), crews carried out dive-bombing exercises (from 5000 feet down to 200 feet) and did much camera work, both vertical pinpoint and oblique photography of recognisable landmarks such as the grandstand at Ascot racecourse. There were take-off and landing sessions with full bomb loads, high-level simulation bombing from 10,000 feet, front and rear-gun live firing at an aluminium marker off-shore near Lyme Bay, and night flying at 15,000 feet practising direction-finding using wireless loop-signals. On one flight with Pilot Officer Lascelles, Tom spent a night at RAF Northolt to take part in an inspection and fly-past for the benefit of a Parliamentary delegation. In June there were night-bombing flights at 10,000 feet, several navigational exercises and simulated bombing raids on Cromer. There were numerous Flight (three aircraft), Squadron (nine) and Wing (twenty-seven) training schedules, as well as Bomber Command tactical manoeuvres, which lasted for hours, flying back and forth over the North Sea coastline to test the radar and anti-aircraft defence systems (see Chapter 11).

By mid-summer, the situation in Europe seemed to be getting much worse, and the airmen sensed that war could start at any time. Half the Squadron was sent on twenty-eight days' leave in July. Tom was one of the lucky ones, for the other half only managed a week when its turn came in August. However, training continued in a concentrated way with Home Defence and Tactical Bombing exercises until the crews felt really confident. They had cause to think seriously about the future though when, in August, all crews had to study the relevant sections of the *War Manual* concerning the rights of prisoners-of-war. It was a little unsettling, too, that they had to parcel up their civilian clothes to be posted home. It made Tom mull over what he had been told on his Gunnery course that, in the First World War, fliers did not survive for much longer than a couple of months. But, in a letter that he sent home on 1 September, as well as promising to make a weekly allotment to his mother, he wrote that the situation looked threatening but 'If anything happens, we'll show them a thing or two.'

Tom's next letter still showed the Harwell address, yet by this time the Wing had been put on a war footing and had flown to Reims in France as part of the Advanced Air Striking Force. On the very next day, 3 September 1939, since the German Chancellor Hitler had failed to respond to Britain's demand that the Germans should leave Poland, war was declared by the Prime Minister, Neville Chamberlain.

Tom was given an additional pilot, Flying Officer Tootal. At first they had very little to do apart from making a few short flights to familiarise themselves with local landmarks. Other squadrons involved in similar reconnaissance flights did not go unpunished; eight aircraft were lost and as many as twenty-four airmen killed on the very first full day of hostilities.

Soon, because Reims was overcrowded with three other squadrons as well as a French one, 105(B) Squadron took up a new station at Villeneuve-les-Vertus near Epernay about 30 miles further south. On 18 September, three aircraft made a reconnaissance flight to check the frontier area. According to Tom, it was entirely nice and peaceful. On 29 September, piloted by P/O Tootal, Tom flew for the first time over German territory with the intention of photographing, from 23,000 feet, the land around Furbach-Lebach. They were made unwelcome and their aircraft was damaged by anti-aircraft fire, but they returned to base safely.

On the following day five Fairey Battles from 150(B) Squadron, on reconnaissance along the border, were lost with the loss of five lives. Since the Fairey Battles flew unescorted, they were easy targets for the German fighters. True, there were some Gloster Gladiator biplane fighters available but they could not even keep up with the German bombers, so they were soon discarded and their pilots sent back to Britain for retraining. There were two squadrons of Hawker Hurricanes stationed at Metz about a hundred miles away, but there were not enough of them to provide adequate protective cover for the bombers, so the reconnaissance flights were ended.

This was the period known as the 'phoney war' or the *sitzkrieg* when nothing much was happening. Yet, in the month of September as many as thirty-nine aircraft were lost and sixty-eight airmen killed. The only bombing of Germany was carried out by Armstrong-Whitworth Whitleys from 4 Group, which dropped tons and tons of propaganda leaflets for the German people to read in the vain hope that they would be convinced of the futility of war.

What was futile was the bombing itself, for even on these peaceful missions, the Whitleys suffered a 6 per cent casualty loss. Propaganda leaflet drops were later coded as 'Nickel' raids. According to some accounts, it seems that 'Bomber' Harris objected to supplying the Germans with enough toilet paper to last the war! The Whitleys used the aerodrome at Villeneuve after the raids because it had the only night-flying facilities near the German border.

In fact, the airfield at Villeneuve could hardly boast of anything else. Most of the aircraft were scattered round the rim, hidden among the trees, which had been thinned out by the airmen themselves. There was one small hangar, which could house just the one plane. The rest of the building accommodated the Station Commander and Flight Commander's offices and the one lavatory that was purpose-built for the use of the whole squadron. So, trenches were dug well away from the huts to be used as open-air lavatories. They had to be disinfected regularly and filled in when fully used – not exactly the height of sophisticated living! Fortunately for the officers and senior NCOs, they were billeted with the French families of Le Mesnil-Sur-Oger, with whom they breakfasted and shared an evening meal. They even had the midday meal delivered to the aerodrome. Some other-rankers were housed in a local brewery. The only complaint they had with this arrangement was that there was no beer to drink, neither in the brewery nor in the village homes, for the French invariably drank wine with every meal. Champagne was freely available at 1s 9d a bottle (about 9p) for, of course, Reims was the marketing centre for Champagne wines.

Aircrews were on stand-by duty permanently, so there were very few opportunities for enjoying free time. Eventually, however, the powers-that-be decided that hanging about waiting for something to happen was not good for morale. A plan was effected for a small operations room to be built underground, and all aircrew and ground staff personnel not directly employed on servicing aircraft had to help. To support and strengthen the underground walls of the pit that had been dug out, empty four-gallon petrol cans were filled with soil and stacked alongside. It turned out that all this work was in vain, though it is interesting to learn that in the 1980s,

Sergeant Hadley (with whom Tom was still in touch) returned to Villeneuve to find that the aerodrome had reverted to arable land. In an attack of curiosity, he went to where he thought that the 'Ops' room had been dug and there, a few inches below the surface, he came across some rusty old cans!

In a letter home, dated 10 December, Tom reported that the station had been visited by the King, presumably with the sincere desire to help maintain the airmen's high spirits. Tom also mentioned that he had received from the local branch of the British Legion a woollen helmet and some handkerchiefs, but that he could do with more regular supplies of daily newspapers so that he could keep abreast of events.

As a further aid to boost morale, it was arranged that a certain number of men could be released each weekend to relax in Paris, which was only about 40 miles distant. Names were drawn out of a hat (life was treated like a lottery) and Costello-Bowen, Sergeant Barnett and Tom were the lucky winners.

They arrived at the Gare de l'Est late at night and managed to find an hotel near the station. On Saturday morning they took the Metro to the Champs Élysées and the Arc de Triomphe. They were in uniform, of course, and they were approached by an English gentleman who welcomed them warmly as the first British servicemen he had encountered in Paris. He was the manager of a Barclays Bank in the city. He invited the three of them to join him for lunch at a first-class restaurant where they were generously feasted. Good food was still plentiful in France. At one café in the Champs Élysées they met Georges Carpentier, perhaps the most famous of all French boxers. Time passed by rapidly and soon they were back in Villeneuve, but whenever they were given the opportunity they would return to this most delightful of cities.

Since there were as many as ten Fairey Battle squadrons in the area, Tom often met quite a few old friends when he went to Epernay to see the films put on by the Army Cinema Unit. On one of the organised trips from Villeneuve, Tom happened to be the sergeant in charge of one lorry-load. On the return journey, the lorry was stopped by a railwayman waving a red lantern. He shouted out that an army lorry returning from Epernay had collided with a train at the level-crossing ahead. Tom's party was the first on the scene, so he had to organise the rescue operation. Despite the prompt response of doctors, ambulancemen and police, about twenty young men were killed and many others seriously injured. Tom himself found three dead soldiers lying in front of the engine. It seemed as if they were just resting, but the horror of their awful sleep still haunts Tom's memory.

As far as flying activity was concerned, there was very little, apart from practice low-level bombing at Moronvilliers, some dummy-attacks on army convoys as part of the Army's and of the RAF's training programme, and a few local and cross-country night-flying exercises. During one operation, the engine in Tom's aircraft blew up and the pilot had to make an emergency wheels-up forced-landing (a pancake landing) on a ploughed field near Hornoy, south-west of Amiens.

In February 1940, during one of the bitterest winters ever recorded, the Squadron was rested for a fortnight at Perpignan, down towards the Spanish border. Here, there was no blackout for the area was well away from the battle zone, there was food and drink in plenty, and the days were sunny and warm. It was sad having to return to Villeneuve, but they did not suffer that much from the icy cold as they were cosily wrapped up in the helmets, gloves, scarves and socks that they had gratefully received from the good people back home who spent so much of their time 'knitting for the Forces'. In his letters home, though, Tom did mention the bitterness of the weather, and said that he was really looking forward to his leave in April.

On 23 April, Mrs Broom noted in her diary that Tom was home on leave. In reality, it became an extended holiday, for the day before Tom was due to return, a visit to the doctor confirmed that he was suffering from German measles (those wretched Germans again), and he could not be allowed to risk infecting others with an illness that could be extremely unpleasant for grown men. After a while, Tom had to report to Uxbridge to be passed fit before returning to active service life in France. In his first letter home after his leave, Tom commented that the French spring had made the countryside absolutely lovely and that if it were not for the war, life would be so wonderful.

In the RAF, Tom had been known as Tommy for a long time.

Somehow it sounded more dashing, and now Tommy adopted a lifestyle that would fit a more cavalier fashion. He had never been a smoker, but having seen so many aircrew puffing away, he decided that he would better look the part if he purchased a pipe for himself. He bought a French pipe and tobacco, and rather enjoyed the new experience. Later on, he received his free ration of St Bruno, the tobacco he favours to this day. At the same time he made up his mind that, being a flying man, it was high time for him to grow a moustache. Even so, May 1940 was more memorable for some other events.

In the previous month, the Germans had invaded and occupied Denmark and Norway with two divisions supported by about 500 combat aircraft and well over 1000 transports. The British tried to disrupt German plans by landing troops at Narvik, but in this first skirmish between them the British force was humiliated, not because of any inadequacy in our infantrymen, but because they were not properly equipped for the task (they did not even have skis to use on the snow-covered slopes of Norway); nor were they adequately supported by planes or heavy artillery. Yet from 11 April to 6 May over fifty bombers were lost with the loss of 170 lives. It seemed as if nothing could deter the overwhelming power of the *Luftwaffe* (Air Force) and the *Wehrmacht* (Army), as had already been witnessed in Czechoslovakia and Poland and now in Norway, so that when they invaded the Low Countries on 10 May, those attacked seemed to yield out of a sense of hopelessness and despair. Tommy remembers that day clearly, for he awoke to the sound of exploding bombs and anti-aircraft fire. Transport arrived to take the crews to the airfield and the Fairey Battles were 'bombed up' in readiness for the order to take off.

During operations that day over Luxembourg, 105(B) Squadron lost four Fairey Battles with one complete crew taken prisoner. LAC McCarthy won the Squadron's first DFM of the war. Tommy remained on site and it was then that he saw his first aerial battle or 'dogfight'. At about 5000 feet, a single Hurricane fighter attacked a formation of Dornier bombers. Unfortunately, it was the lone hero who was shot down. That night, Tommy retired to the Mess to drink the frustration out of his system, for he had been more than ready to go into action. It so happened that he had to wait rather longer, for his pilot, Sergeant Costello-Bowen, had caught a severe cold and was forbidden to fly until he had recovered. With hindsight, Tommy realises that he was one of the lucky ones. Kind fate kept him from being a statistic in the 50 per cent loss of aircrew suffered by 105(B) Squadron during the Battle for France.

Although the Fairey Battle was a vast improvement on the old Hart and Hardy biplanes, it was already an anachronism in terms of aerial warfare. It was far too slow and cumbersome to evade German fighters. It could only carry a 1000-pound bomb load over a comparatively short distance. Of the RAF's medium bombers, the Vickers Wellington and the Bristol Blenheim were just about adequate to attack German targets, but the Handley Page Hampden and the Armstrong-Whitworth Whitley were so ineffective that they were rapidly transferred to other duties. To make matters worse, the German pilots were battle-hardened as, only a few months earlier, they had benefited from considerable aggressive flying in the Spanish Civil War. They knew about fighter-to-fighter combat, and about providing close support for ground troops. In fact, the Condor Legion had only been abandoned three months before the outbreak of hostilities in September 1939. Therefore, from the very beginning, British losses were heavy, not only of aircraft but, much worse, of pre-war trained aircrews – the most experienced men in the RAF. All these factors combined to convince the airmen that their bombers were fit for museums only and, indeed, they were tragically proven to be right in May 1940.

In under a week the RAF lost four Hampdens, a Whitley, fifty-eight Blenheims and eighty-one Battles, as well as all twelve Westland Lysander spotter-planes. Even worse, 152 experienced fliers lost their lives and a further seventy were made prisoners-of-war. Over the Albert Canal, five out of six volunteer Battle crews from 12 Squadron were lost, and it was little consolation to learn that the RAF's first Victoria Crosses of the war had been awarded posthumously to Flying Officer Garland (the pilot) and Sergeant Gray (the observer). For some unfathomable reason, the air-gunner (LAC Reynolds) was not similarly honoured. Tommy's 105(B) Squadron lost seven out of eleven Battles with twelve airmen killed and three made prisoners-of-war at the Sedan bridges, but no matter how many bridges were destroyed, they were soon replaced by pontoon bridges to carry the German armies across the River Meuse. On 17 May, eleven Blenheims and twenty-two airmen from 82 Squadron based at RAF Watton were lost.

By the end of May, the Fairey Battle had been discounted as a feasible daylight bomber. Indeed, since well over half the bomber force had been shot down either by fighters or by 'flak' (*Flugabwehrkanone*) the War Cabinet was most reluctant to send more squadrons to France. Whatever the ultimate cost had been, of one thing there is no doubt, not enough tribute was paid to the brave pilots, observers and air-gunners who flew to almost certain death in Fairey Battles during those bitter days of 1940.

In the meantime, Holland had surrendered and Brussels had been captured. There were twelve million refugees on the roads of France as the Germans advanced 200 miles in a week. It was these heavily defended and rapidly advancing columns of troops and tanks that the Fairey Battle squadrons had been expected to destroy or, at least, delay. Each Battle was armed with a front-firing machine-gun, another one for the air-gunner, and one fixed to the belly of the plane to be used by the observer/bomb-aimer. For added protection, the observer sat on a small piece of armour-plate. Tommy warned his less-experienced colleagues to stay on the armour-plate and avoid the natural inclination to crane their heads out to get a better view of the action below. Tommy's old friend, Sergeant Hadley, for many years bought him a slap-up meal as a token of gratitude for that advice. In the raid on the Sedan bridges, anti-aircraft fire ripped his gun off, and if he had been leaning over he would not have lived to tell the tale. He and his pilot, Flying Officer Gibson, did crash, however, and were made prisoners-of-war. Flying Officer Gibson managed to escape and eventually reached Allied lines safely, but was shot down again when flying on a Lancaster operation in 1943. Sergeant Hadley remained a prisoner until May 1945, five years in captivity altogether.

By the middle of May, the situation in France was getting desperate. The German army had reached the River Aisne, which was only about 20 miles away from Villeneuve. There were now only two aircraft operational in the Squadron, so Tommy's crew and another were instructed to fly the Battles to comparative safety at Romilly-sur-Seine, where they would receive further orders. The crews were not allowed to drive back to their village billets to collect their belongings, so they lost all their possessions in the hurried evacuation. At Romilly, Tommy met the remnants of 501 Fighter Squadron, which had been stationed at Filton before the war, not all that far from Portishead. They had had a rough time, as had so many Hurricane squadrons. Altogether, of the 261 Hurricanes that had been deployed in France (including the last-minute reinforcements), seventy-five had been shot down or were too seriously damaged to be repaired, 120 had had to be destroyed to prevent them from falling into enemy hands, and sixty-six only were left to be flown back to defend Britain.

Before long, an Air Commodore arrived at Romilly. He ordered the two crews to fly the Battles to a landing-ground at Eschemine near Troyes. There, they were to hand over the planes to 12 Squadron. The rest of the Squadron arrived later by motor transport. Fortunately, the Germans had not pushed south to Reims, but used the River Aisne to guard their left flank as they swung north-west towards the Channel ports. This was a lucky escape for the retreating airmen. By the end of May, Belgium had capitulated and the ports of Calais and Boulogne had been captured. There were 500,000 troops on the beaches of Northern France being pounded by the Germans. By 4 June, when Dunkirk fell, 330,000 men had been evacuated, saved to fight another day by the Royal Navy and hundreds of little ships, many of them manned by civilian volunteers. Altogether, in the Battle for France, the RAF had lost over 900 aircraft. By 10 June, Paris had fallen and, within a week, France sought an Armistice. On 16 July in Directive No. 16, Hitler ordered landing operations to obliterate the English motherland as a military base, and to occupy the country completely. Three days later, he issued a 'last appeal to reason', hoping that the British would sue for peace.

As all this was going on, Tommy's squadron had entrained for, and had eventually reached, Nantes on the west coast, where they camped under canvas until early June anxiously awaiting their next move. The air-gunners were posted to other squadrons, so that many friendships were broken, indeed ended, for later on, many of them lost their lives at sea. Almost 6000 servicemen and civilians had been crammed on to HM Troopship *Lancastria* (a Cunard liner that normally accommodated 2000 passengers) at St Nazaire on 17 June. She had hardly started on her voyage when she was dive-bombed by German aircraft. One bomb went down the funnel and blew a large hole in the ship. She sank rapidly to the sea-bed and almost 5000 of those on board were drowned, the single biggest loss of British lives in the war. It was not until the war had ended that information about the disaster was made public, for the Government feared that news of such a tragedy on top of the heavy defeat in France would surely be a blow to national morale.

The airmen left at Nantes were split up into small sections of ten men, each group being the responsibility of a sergeant. In this way, roll-calls could be carried out promptly. Tommy got to know his group very well (and vice-versa) on the train journey to Cherbourg – in old wagons that had been used in the First World War to carry forty troops or eight horses! As they moved north-east, the French people thought that they were on their way to the front line, so they were welcomed generously with food and wine at every stop on the way. At Cherbourg, three days before it was captured by the Germans, after much to-ing and fro-ing from one quayside to another, at last they boarded a former cross-Channel ferry, which took them safely overnight to a home port. At Southampton, they were temporarily housed and fed in a large harbour shed before they left for an unknown destination. When they reached Bury St Edmunds they were immediately taken by lorry to RAF Honington. On the following day, they were medically examined, pronounced fit, and given a week's leave, so ending a depressing few months. It seemed as if the war situation was hopeless. Most of Europe had been conquered by the ever victorious German armies and, now, Britain itself would be hammered into submission by the *Luftwaffe*'s massive bombing campaign (or so the Germans assumed).

Portishead, because of its proximity to Bristol and Avonmouth Docks and, indeed, because of its own small dock and power station, was not immune to attack. It was also vulnerable to chance raids from aircraft bombing shipping in the Channel or mine-laying. In her diary, Mrs Broom recorded faithfully the regular bombing during 1940 and well into 1941. On most days she mentioned the wailing of sirens, going in and out of shelters and the incessant droning of German planes above until, eventually, the feeling of apprehension was replaced by a sense of boredom. Even when bombs were dropped on the neighbouring small villages of Portbury, Pill, Clapton and Wraxall, the incidents were noted as if they were of no great significance. More notice was taken when four residents were killed in Albert Road exactly a year to the day that war was declared. There was a sense of justice done when, in the same month, a Heinkel 111 (one of a force attacking the airfield and factory at Filton) was hit by anti-aircraft fire from 236 Battery stationed at Portbury. It crashed into a ploughed field at Racecourse Farm between Failand and Portbury. The five members of the crew baled out safely and were made prisoners-of-war. From his new posting at RAF Watton in Norfolk, Tom wrote home to express concern about his parents' safety and to wish them a few quiet nights' rest. In January 1941, Christ Church at Pill was destroyed by incendiary bombs, and a high-explosive bomb dropped between Clapton-in-Gordano and Portbury made a crater 60 feet across and 30 feet deep. In February, three mines were dropped off Battery Point, one of which did not explode

In April 1941, when the heaviest raids were carried out, a Heinkel 111 was set on fire above Portishead by a Beaufighter from RAF Middle Wallop. It crashed in flames at Hewish, between Clevedon and Weston-super-Mare. On 11 April (Good Friday) the centre of Bristol was pretty well demolished. On the same night, bombs fell on the harbour at Portishead and behind the Quakers' Chapel in St Mary's Road (where Gordano School is now). As the night went on, high-explosive bombs fell on the Power Station, the Albion Inn in Bristol Road, Clapton Lane, Woodland Road, the old Rectory paddock and the Paper Mills. There was damage to gas, water and electricity services, and the High Street was blocked by debris from the bombing. From German records, it seems that as many as seventeen aircraft concentrated their attack on Old Posset, thirty-six targeted Avonmouth and ninety-eight Bristol.

The gloom was brightened considerably for Mrs Broom when her children came home. By this time, as well as Tom serving with the RAF (he was still Tom at home, not Tommy, though his village friends were wont to address him as Broomy), Bob was with the Lothians and Border Yeomanry, Peter belonged to a searchlight battery attached to RAF Hullavington near Chippenham, and

Muriel was working at an underground factory at Corsham near Bath.

No one could question the loyalty of the Broom family at Rhondda Villas. At one time, Peter was stationed at Battery Point itself when he served with 365 Coastal Battery, a most comfortable posting it would seem but, perhaps, not all that safe, for local people claimed that some of the war's first bombs to drop on English soil fell on the foreshore there in June 1940. In the very next month, a Junkers 88 (bombing ships in the Channel) and a Heinkel 111 (mine-laying) were both attacked over Portishead and crashed, eventually, somewhere in Devon.

CHAPTER 5

The Way Things Were

Nowadays, despite political misunderstandings, the occasional outburst of excessive patriotism and the events in the Middle East that remind us of how viciously intolerant ethnic groups can be, the peoples of Europe live together in relative peace. Even in circumstances when our military forces have been deployed (often with the disapproval of the British people, in the Falklands and in Iraq in particular) our country's safety and well-being was not directly threatened except in a vague way, and our daily lives continued in an uninterrupted fashion. Despite some terror attacks in London, it may be difficult for present generations to appreciate, over sixty years later, how much the British were united in their fear of the evil that was threatening them from across the Channel in 1940.

The *Luftwaffe* had gained a dreadful reputation with its callous bombing of innocent civilians at Guernica in 1937 during the Spanish Civil War (a tragedy made famous by Picasso), at Warsaw in 1939 when Poland was attacked without warning, and at Rotterdam in 1940, which, undefended, suffered 30,000 civilian casualties. These were early examples of how German warfare easily deteriorated into terrorism. The seemingly irresistible *Luftwaffe* had at its disposal 3530 operational aircraft and 500 transport planes. It would have been foolish indeed for the people of this country not to have been afraid. What was magnificent was how they responded, and stood alone with courage and tenacity against a conscienceless enemy. As Winston Churchill pronounced, it was to be their finest hour. It should be remembered that though the Americans and the Russians eventually provided the power that was necessary to defeat the Nazis, they did not become involved in the conflict until much later, the Americans almost a year and a half later, when their naval base at Pearl Harbor was attacked by

Japanese forces. Of course, whereas previously the fighting had been to support and protect other nations across the Channel, now the British people had to be ready to defend themselves and the things they held most dear.

Already in 1940, the people of Britain had undergone much discomfort in preparing for the invasion that was bound to come, and the heavy bombing that would accompany it. Children had been traumatically separated from their families and evacuated to the countryside. People who were too old or infirm to be in the Forces became Fire Watchers, Air-Raid Wardens, Air Observers and Home Guardsmen. Men, women and children became accustomed to seeing pill-boxes, anti-tank barriers, barbed-wire entanglements, sandbagged doors and windows, Anderson shelters (named after the Government minister responsible), and anti-aircraft barrage balloons everywhere, and to not seeing signposts and name-plates, which had been dismantled with the intention of bewildering the invading armies. They got used to carrying gas masks, identity cards and ration books. They learned to react quickly to air-raid sirens and, at night, to put up black-out curtains to hide all household lights from the aeroplanes above.

By the end of summer 1940, Germany was in control of the whole of mainland Europe or, if not in direct control, certainly exercised such powerful influence on neighbouring smaller countries that it could claim to be master of the continent. The German Third Reich and its dominant Nazi regime had gained this superiority through a combination of superb, grandiose showmanship, diplomatic deception and everyday ruthless terror.

Within Germany itself, there was a permanent state of emergency, with the all-powerful, one-party-state in absolute control. Liberty of a kind, if it existed at all, was dependent on blind and total obedience to authority, the authority of the *Führer* (Leader). For the vast majority of Germans, this was a situation of utter contentment and they felt patriotically proud of their military prowess. But for those who could not or would not conform (or in any way offended the Nazi code of racial purity), concentration camps were built to accommodate them and, eventually, to be the locations for their wholesale murder.

As early as 1934, just a year after he had been elected to office by the German people, Hitler ordered the execution of some of his oldest and most loyal friends, including Ernst Rohm, the head of the SA (the Brownshirts), the organisation that had done most to secure power for him. Other old comrades were murdered, no matter how close they had been to him in the past. Even heroes with Iron Crosses who had fought bravely in the First World War for Germany, but who were found to have traces of Jewish blood, were sent to their deaths in concentration camps. Within Germany then, official sanction was given for murder to be a normal, almost legal, process for ridding the state of unwanted or 'anti-social' elements, that is, all political opponents and any peoples regarded as racially inferior, classified according to Nazi philosophy as *unter-menschen*. If the Nazis were capable of such horrifying deeds against their own countrymen, how much more vicious could they be when dealing with the defeated inhabitants of conquered territories – lands occupied to provide the German people with *lebensraum* (living space).

Obergruppenführer Reinhard Heydrich was deputy chief of the SS (*Schutzstaffel*) and of the *Gestapo* (*Geheime Staatspolizei*) under Himmler. He was also chief of the Security Police and the Protector of Bohemia and Moravia (Czechoslovakia). Heydrich was feared in the occupied territories for his utter lack of humanity and known as 'Hangman Heydrich'. He was attacked in Prague at the end of May 1942 by two Free Czech agents who had been parachuted into the country by the British. Heydrich died of his wounds about a week later. To teach the Czechoslovakians a lesson, and as a threat to all conquered peoples, the Germans embarked on a campaign of violent terror. Over a thousand Czechs (including 200 women) were immediately executed. A hundred people or more sought refuge in the Karl Borromaeus Church, but they were killed. The two agents, Jan Kubis and Josef Gabeik, were amongst those hiding there. The village of Lidice, near Prague, was surrounded by units of the Security Police. No one was allowed to leave. A mother, fearful for the safety of her son, tried to flee. Both were shot. Anyone who wished to enter the village was allowed in without question. The entire male population was locked in some barns and stables. From the dawning of 10 June (a beautiful summer's day just before the hay harvest), until 4 o'clock in the afternoon, the men were taken out in batches of ten or so and murdered by a Secret Police firing squad in front of their loved ones. Altogether, nearly 200 men and boys were killed. Following the massacre, some 200 women and ninety children were sent to concentration camps, from which few managed to leave alive. Seven women found near the village were taken to Prague and shot. Four pregnant women were taken to a maternity hospital, but their babies were murdered as soon as they were born and their mothers imprisoned in concentration camps. The village of Lidice was burnt to the ground, the buildings dynamited and the rubble levelled so that no trace remained. Elsewhere, 3000 Jews were shipped in cattle-trucks to be exterminated and, in Berlin, 150 of the remaining Jews in the city suffered a similar fate.

On 10 June 1944, exactly two years later, the villagers of Oradour-sur-Glane, near Limoges in France, were accused of having hidden explosives. A German SS Division (the *Das Reich*, which had gained a reputation for terror, if not courage, in Russia) imprisoned the men and shepherded the women and children into the village church. The barns in which the men were kept were set on fire. Those who tried to escape were shot. The women and children heard the firing of machine-guns and knew that their fathers, husbands, brothers and sons were lost to them for ever. They waited in fear until the German soldiers came to kill them too. As many as 650 villagers were massacred. The charred bodies of fifteen little children were found heaped up behind the burnt out altar of the church. By pretending to be dead for long enough, ten women and children survived to tell the tale.

Lidice and Oradour-sur-Glane are memorials to the martyrdom of innocent men, women and children. Babi Yar in the Ukraine, Palmiry in Poland, Televaag in Norway, and villages in Greece, Yugoslavia and Belorussia suffered similar atrocities. In the last months of 1941 alone, half a million Russian Jews were slaughtered. One *Einsatzgruppen* unit boasted of murdering 90,000 men, women and children during that year.

If the invasion of Britain in September 1940 had succeeded, Heydrich would have commanded the Reich Central Security Office in London. Six *Einsatzcommando* units were to operate from London, Bristol, Birmingham, Liverpool, Manchester and

Edinburgh to implement his orders. *Einsatzcommando* units had a peculiar responsibility for carrying out 'special missions'. They used stark terror to control occupied territory and to subjugate the people. For these units, the massacre of blameless civilians rated as of no more significance than any other daily task. Murder and other more refined cruelties were simply part of normal routine. Himmler, the supreme head of the SS and one of Hitler's most trusted deputies, once praised his troops for remaining clean, decent men despite their murderous work! Heydrich's first instructions to the *Einsatzcommandos* were to arrest, intern and then dispatch to the continent all able-bodied men aged seventeen to forty-five years to provide skilled slave-labour in German factories and farms. Those remaining had to conform and obey orders – or else. All property of value was to be confiscated and, whenever and wherever needed, hostages were to be taken into custody. Failure to hand in weapons and radio-sets was punishable by immediate execution. Anyone showing the slightest antagonism towards the occupying forces, for example by displaying notices or posters that were offensive to them, would suffer the same fate. SS *Hauptsturmführer* Otto Begus, with a task force of a hundred paratroopers, was commanded to seize the King, Queen and the two Princesses and hold them hostage to guarantee a speedy end to all opposition.

The man who was to be Heydrich's deputy in Britain, SS Colonel Dr Franz Six, served instead in Russia a year later. The *Einsatzgruppen* under his immediate command committed atrocities and wholesale massacres daily. If Britain had been occupied in 1940, one wonders what would have been the fate of millions of Britons. What then, dear Old Posset? Would there have been minor incidents of opposition, or even serious instances of outright rebellion to cause the German occupying force to exact vengeance? What would have happened to Bill and Ena Norman? They were well-known and much-loved residents, and gifted musicians both. When the war was over, they went to a lot of trouble to identify and to write a sympathetic letter to the parents of a German airman who had lost his life over Portishead. His Heinkel 111 had been shot down by anti-aircraft fire directed from a gun-battery stationed at Portbury. The aircraft crashed into the water between Portbury Wharf and Avonmouth, some hundreds of yards from the Royal

Hotel, on 22 February 1941. Bert Metcalf, who worked at the power station then, had been ordered to go to the air-raid shelter but, being curious, he took the lift up to the top to see more clearly what was happening. He remembers, as if it had happened only yesterday, how the plane went round in circles, gradually losing height until, eventually, it crashed into the mouth of the River Avon. Bob Ferriman, just back from Saturday morning lessons at Bristol Cathedral School, waded on to the mud flats, found a pistol (which was immediately confiscated by the Navy), slipped on the mud and ruined his school uniform. The young airman who was killed was buried in the cemetery at North Weston but later reinterred at the German war-graves cemetery at Cannock Chase in Staffordshire. When Bill and Ena celebrated their Golden Wedding at the Somerset Hall in the village, the airman's mother and sister came as surprise guests to express their gratitude for the kindness shown them. Yet Bill and Ena, both fine and stalwart Posset people, might not have lived long enough to show such generosity if Portishead had been under the command of an *Hauptsturmführer* from 1940 onwards. As a further tragic reminder of the bitter futility of war, of the Heinkel's crew no trace could be found of two of the young fliers, but many years later some human bones were found trapped in the filters of the second Portishead power station.

What seems to be, on first reading, a somewhat florid tribute by the American people to the men and women of Bristol and Britain, in truth expressed the warm-hearted feelings of people everywhere in those dark days. A plaque unveiled in June 1942 recorded proudly:

> *BRISTOL BASIN*
> *BENEATH THIS EAST RIVER*
> *DRIVE OF THE CITY OF NEW YORK*
> *LIE STONES, BRICKS AND RUBBLE*
> *FROM THE BOMBED CITY OF BRISTOL*
> *IN ENGLAND. BROUGHT HERE IN*
> *BALLAST FROM OVERSEAS, THESE*
> *FRAGMENTS THAT ONCE WERE HOMES*
> *SHALL TESTIFY WHILE MEN LOVE*
> *FREEDOM TO THE RESOLUTION AND*

FORTITUDE OF THE PEOPLE OF BRITAIN.
THEY SAW THEIR HOMES STRUCK DOWN
WITHOUT WARNING. IT WAS NOT
THEIR HOMES BUT THEIR VALOR
THAT KEPT THEM FREE.
And broad-based under all
Is planted England's oaken-hearted mood
As rich in fortitude
As e'er went worldward from the island wall.

Erected by the
ENGLISH-SPEAKING UNION OF THE UNITED STATES
1942

CHAPTER SIX

Europe Revisited

Tommy's 105 Squadron moved to RAF Watton in Norfolk in July 1940, where 21 and 82 Squadrons were already stationed. They, also, had suffered grievous losses in daylight raids on heavily defended German armoured columns during the Battle for France. Within a few days of losing all but one of its aircraft, 82 Squadron, led by the legendary Wing Commander the Earl of Bandon (Paddy or the A-bandon-ed Earl), acquired six new Blenheims and returned to action immediately. Now, it was the turn of 105 Squadron to receive replacement aircraft, Blenheims (Mk IV) instead of the Battles. It also received new crews, in particular air-gunners to compensate for the losses sustained during the evacuation from France. Paddy Bandon, a happy hail-fellow well-met sort of hero, took an interest. Sitting cross-legged on the crew-room table, as if he were 'one of the lads' rather than a Wing Commander, he gave several talks on how to handle Blenheims. Tommy remembers him with affection as a glittering character, whose departure from 82 Squadron was regretted by all at RAF Watton.

Fresh crews were formed and Tommy linked up once more with Sergeant Costello-Bowen (Flying Officer Tootal had been taken off flying duties because of illness) but with a new gunner, Sergeant Evans. They first flew as a crew on 17 July and then spent the rest of the month training, much of it formation-flying at low level across country, and carrying out some bomb-aiming practice over Wainfleet.

By the first week of August, 105 Squadron was considered fit to go into action against the enemy. The first two operations were to Knocke in Belgium, but as there was no cloud cover they returned to base as commanded. Because of unsustainable heavy losses suffered during daylight raids, instructions had been issued only to attack if there was adequate cloud cover. In fact, during July, 90 per cent of daylight raids were aborted because of clear skies.

On 10 August, the new crew attacked the aerodrome at Flushing. There was some flak, but the only damage inflicted was to a Henschel 126, one of the enemy's own planes that happened to be in the vicinity. Back safely, the crew went to Norwich to celebrate their first real action together. It was not the only time that they would be found drinking at the 'Castle' or at the 'Samson and Hercules'.

As there was an expectation of imminent invasion, some regional control exercises were carried out. Tommy, piloted by Wing Commander Hawtrey, took part in a square-search operation round the area of the aerodrome to check for signs pointing to the airfield, such as arrow-heads cut in fields of corn by fifth-columnists (secret German agents). During August, all bomber squadrons were given a length of coastline to supervise – 105 Squadron's was North Somercotes, a long stretch of sand between Grimsby and Skegness on the Lincolnshire coast. Dummy bombing runs were made as preparation for the real thing should German landing-craft attempt to beach there. Also in August, the Squadron spent a day at RAF Northolt giving a Canadian fighter squadron some necessary experience before its pilots took part in aerial combat. Before very long their skilful handling of Hurricanes was to be tested in the Battle of Britain.

In the late summer and autumn months of 1940, with Britain alone and dangerously exposed, the Germans planned to take advantage of their perceived superiority to mount an invasion, code-named Seelowe (Sea Lion).

In a speech to the Reichstag, Hitler said that he was prepared to give Britain a last opportunity to sue for peace. Copies of his speech, which were dropped as leaflets on this country, were auctioned in aid of 'Red Cross Funds'! When Hitler realised that his offer had been contemptuously rejected, he ordered that the plans for Sea Lion should be given the highest priority, and that the Channel crossing should be made on 15 September.

In order to transport approximately 300,000 troops, a few divisions of armoured vehicles and essential supplies across the narrow stretch of water, over 1000 invasion craft (mainly large barges but with some freighters and trawlers) were assembled in

1. Tom (on the right) with two fellow recruits Gerry Hart and Fred Powar during their first fortnight in the R.A.F.

2. RAF Abingdon R.U. XV, Tom is the first on the left in the front row.

3. The Armourers' X1 at R.A.F. Eastchurch, Tom is in the middle of the front row.

4. 'A' Flight No 47(B) Squadron in front of a Vickers Vincent 1936-37. Tommy is 3rd from left in the back row.

5. 47(B) Squadron at RAF Khartoum in 1937.

9. Tom in 1939.

8. Peter and Tom in July 1940.

7. Tom is having a break after 'bombing up' four Hawker Harts in 1938. His knees are grubby from kneeling on the ground. The inverted stripe on his left sleeve represented 3 years' Good Conduct, and entitled him to a pay rise of 3d a day (1½p).

6. Armament Section, 47(B) Squadron, Khartoum 1937. Tom is the sun-tanned airman in the rear rank.

10. Sgts. Costello-Bowen and Broom with their Blenheim.

11. This miniaturised copy of a page taken from Tommy's Log Book is of special interest for it reports what happened on the 26th of November 1940 after the attack on the railway yards at Cologne.

12. Tom and his brother Bob who was later killed in action in North Africa.

13. Ivor and Tommy with the ground crew that kept their 'Crossed Broomsticks' Mosquito (MM118) in good trim. The two of them flew this aircraft on 24 bombing raids, all from the RAF station at Oakington in summer 1944.

14. The Flying Brooms.

15. HMS *Malaya,* the ship on which Tommy was returned to England from Gibraltar after his escape.

163 SQUADRON PARTY

THE OFFICERS N.C.O's & AIRMEN OF Nº 163 SQUADRON REQUEST THE PLEASURE OF YOUR COMPANY AT A SQU......... ...ARTY TO BE HELD IN THE UPPE..... ...NG HALL ON COMM...... .....G AT 2000HRS.

17. To one Thomas Broom, Spiritual and Cultural leader of Squadron No.128 from the members of 1409 Flight.

"It burst in bounteous raggedness,
From whence no man can tell
Quite seasonless, a lovely growth
In winter's icy spell."

18. 165 Squadron in March 1945.

... 165 SQUADRON MARCH 1945...

19. VE Day celebrations.

20. Officers of 163(B) Squadron. The Flying Brooms centre.

Date	Time	Aircraft	Pilot	Duty	Remarks		
/8	1600	MM 118	F/Lt Broom	NAV	N.F.T		35
/8	2210	MM 118	F/Lt Broom	OPERATIONS.	WANNE EICKEL (RUHR) 28000. 4 x 500lb		2·40
8.	1550	MM 118	F/Lt Broom	NAV.	N.F.T	40	
8	1130	MM 118	F/Lt Broom	NAV.	N.F.T & PRACTICE BOMBING	50	
8	2158	MM 118	F/Lt Broom	OPERATIONS.	COLOGNE. 26,000' 1 x 4000lb		3·00
8	0134	MM 118	F/Lt Broom	OPERATIONS ⊕	GARDENING. DORTMUND-EMS CANAL. Low level		2·45
8.	2128	MM 118	F/Lt Broom	OPERATIONS.	BERLIN. 27500 1 x 4000lb		4·15
/8	2155	MM 118	F/Lt Broom	OPERATIONS	BERLIN 28000 1 x 4000 lb		4·15
/8	1135	MM 145	F/Lt Broom	BOMBING	MK XIV 25000'	1·35	
/8	1505	MM 118	F/Lt Broom	NAV	N.F.T	15	
/8	2226	MM 118	F/Lt Broom	OPERATIONS.	BERLIN. 27000' 1 x 4000lb A/c Lit A/c Flak		4·25
/8	1520	MM 186	F/Lt Broom.	NAV	N.F.T	15	
/8	2211	MM 186	F/Lt Broom	OPERATIONS	MANNHEIM 25000' 1 x 4000lb	3·20	
/8	1535	PF 381.	F/Lt Broom	NAV.	N.F.T	30	
/8	2349	PF 383.	F/Lt Broom	OPERATIONS	BERLIN 28000' 1 x 4000lb		4·15
/8	1536	MM 115	F/Lt Broom	NAV.	N.F.T.	15	
/8	2210	MM 115	F/Lt Broom	OPERATIONS	DÜSSELDORF 27000' 1 x 4000lb		3·05

TOTAL TIME | 811·00 | 162·00

21. Tommy's August 1944 Log Book entry was as concise as his mother's note in her diary had been, but with the addition of one seemingly incongruous word - 'gardening'. This referred to the 'planting' of 'cucumbers', a laconic way of describing a mine-laying attack.

BAR TO D.F.C.

AWARD TO PORTISHEAD AIRMAN

A Portishead airman is one of two "Brooms sweeping the air" in the news today.

He is Flt. Lt. Thos. John Broom (30), eldest son of Mr. and Mrs. J. Broom, 2, Rhondda Villas, Slade Rd., Portishead, and he receives a Bar to his D.F.C. for exploits which are at present "hush-hush."

In the same squadron — No. 128, R.A.F. — is Actg. Sqdn.-Ldr. Ivor G. Broom, of Glamorgan, and an award to him is also announced — a second Bar to his D.F.C.

Flt. Lt. Broom entered the R.A.F. over 12 years ago and was commissioned in 1942. In the same year he was reported missing after an operational flight, but, after experiencing many hazards, he was picked up by a ship and landed at Gibraltar a month later.

He received his D.F.C. last August. One brother is in the Army and another was killed in action in North Africa.

22. The reason for the award was kept secret, and the newspaper reports made no reference to the Kaiserslautern tunnel. Nor did the press indicate how out of the ordinary it was for a pilot to win three gallantry awards, and how even more unusual it was for a navigator to win two.

Bristol Evening World & Eveni...

'Hush-hush' Award to Portishead Airman

Acting-Squadron-Leader Ivor Gordon Broom, of Glamorgan, and Acting-Flight-Lieut. Thomas John Broom, of Portishead, both belong to No. 128 R.A.F. Squadron.

Both were commissioned from the ranks and both are included in R.A.F. awards to-day. Sqdn.-Ldr. Broom receives the second bar to the D.F.C., while Flt.-Lt. Broom gets the bar to the D.F.C.

Both awards are "Hush, hush" —no details are given of the recipients' exploits.

Flt.-Lt. Broom also wears the 1939-43 Star.

23. Squadron Leader Tommy Broom earthbound towards the end of the war.

25. Tommy enjoys the family life after his return from post-war Germany.

26. Tommy and Bertie 'The Boy' Boulter at Swanton Morley in front of Bertie's Stearman.

27. The Queen Mother chats to Ivor Broom, with Tommy looking on behind the royal feathers, during the Pathfinder reunion during 1984.

28. Air Commodore T.E.A. Sismore DSO DFC** AFC, Air Marshal Sir Ivor Broom DSO DFC** AFC, F/Lt George Robson DFC* and S/Ldr Tommy Broom DFC**. Four distinguished and heroic low-level operators relaxing in Sir Ivor's garden – maybe in their maturer years, but still appropriately armed!

29. Tommy at the 1992 Pathfinder Reunion at RAF Wyton.

30. Pathfinders at the Four Horseshoes Inn after the 1992 Reunion.

31. Pathfinder Sunday 2006 at RAF Wyton.

32. The legendary Squadron Leader Tommy Broom DFC**

the Channel ports of France, Belgium and Holland. Another 1500 river barges and pleasure-boats were commandeered to provide a proper back-up. There was a rapid build-up. For example, in Ostend in the first four days of September, the number of barges increased from eighteen to over 200. It was estimated that it would take a whole day for such an armada to cross the Channel, and four more days to secure a bridgehead along a narrow coastal strip in Kent and Sussex. To guarantee success, the operation would require overwhelming air superiority, not only to overcome the expected RAF response but, also, to attack the Royal Navy, which would certainly gather to dispute control of the English Channel.

Reichsmarschall Hermann Goering, commander of the *Luftwaffe*, was confident that his overwhelmingly superior force would be victorious. Whereas the RAF had about 700 operational fighter aircraft, the *Luftwaffe* had some 1000 fighters, 1000 medium bombers and 250 dive-bombers. *Adlertag* (Eagle Day) was to be on 10 August but, because of bad weather, it was delayed for a couple of days. The *Luftwaffe* concentrated its strength in the Pas de Calais area so that its bombers and fighters would have the maximum flying time possible over England. British shipping, especially convoys bringing food and war material into the country, were dive-bombed relentlessly, and the south-eastern counties were so remorselessly attacked that the area around Dover and Folkestone became known as 'Hellfire Corner'. However, the *Luftwaffe*'s main task was to make the RAF ineffective. Airfields were to be the priority targets, with low-level bombing and strafing used to destroy the fighter squadrons on the ground, or to catch aircraft as they came in to land having used up their fuel and ammunition. Six airfields were made unusable almost immediately, but what was much more devastating was that as well as a few hundred planes destroyed, over a hundred fighter pilots were killed and many more seriously injured. As a senior officer was reported to have said, the survival of Britain would depend on the Royal Navy and a thousand or so pink-cheeked young airmen. There is no doubt that the air battle was won by the unflinching courage of exhausted young men who had gathered from the Empire, the countries of Occupied Europe, the USA and Britain itself. By the end of August, so severe were the losses that many of the pilots left to fight were quite inexperienced, but they were, thankfully, dashing, carefree youngsters who never gave up.

By this time, then, Fighter Command was on its knees. What helped to save the situation was that Britain possessed a radar system. The information gathered was fed to a coordinating centre and then distributed to the various fighter stations so that squadrons would take off as soon as German bombers were reported to be massing over Calais. In this way, no time was wasted searching for the bomber fleets in the skies. An even greater advantage was that, whereas the protective cover of German fighters could spend about ten minutes over England before their fuel ran out, the defending Hurricanes and Spitfires, newly refuelled, could stay aloft long enough to attack the now unprotected Dorniers, Junkers and Heinkels. The *Luftwaffe* was prevented from gaining the superiority that it sought and, even more frustrating for the Germans, they did not detect any weakening of British resolve. When they realised that an invasion was unlikely to succeed, Sea Lion was abandoned, and Hitler became more and more obsessed with his long-cherished ambition of moving eastwards against Russia.

A great deal has been written about the Battle of Britain when 'so much was owed by so many to so few' to quote Winston Churchill's warm tribute to the brave fighter pilots. It should not be forgotten that the equally brave Bomber Command pilots, observers and air-gunners shared in the glory as they persistently attacked the Channel ports of Dunkirk, Boulogne, Calais, Ostend and Dieppe (collectively known as 'Blackpool Front') and German airfields, continuing despite horrendous losses.

It soon became evident that Blenheim crews on low-level daylight raids were involved in the most dangerous RAF operations of the war. Flying sometimes at just over 50 feet above ground, the planes had to go through a concentrated barrage of flak. They could be fired on from the front, from the side, from behind and from below. The Blenheims were vulnerable to fighter attack as well, for they flew unescorted on these missions. The losses were frightening at times. In an attack on an airfield in Denmark to destroy Junkers transports and bombers massing in readiness for the invasion, the entire 82 Squadron was shot down. (This was the very same squadron that had been battered during the Battle for France.) It is not often acknowledged that during the Battle of Britain Bomber Command lost more aircrew than Fighter Command. The three airmen in a Blenheim, taking part in a low-level operation, had little chance of escaping both flak and fighters. Though pilots loved its versatility and its flying and handling characteristics, the Blenheim was too slow (with a maximum speed of 250 mph) for daylight bombing raids and was certainly no match for the Messerschmitt 109s and 110s. Yet, despite the 50 per cent loss rate or, perhaps, because of it, the crews maintained a fine spirit of comradeship, and they carried out their tasks with determination and skill. The following year, when Churchill visited RAF Swanton Morley, he praised the Blenheim crews of 105 Squadron with the words, 'The Charge of the Light Brigade at Balaclava is eclipsed in brightness by these daily deeds of fame.' Yet, when Tommy took part in a daylight raid on Hingene aerodrome in Belgium, he reported no fighters and very little flak. That Saturday, they were back celebrating in Norwich.

Bomber Command played an equally crucial, though accidental, role in persuading the Germans to modify their strategy. Berlin was to be attacked – a sort of goaded response to the *Luftwaffe*'s bombing campaign. At the briefing beforehand, crews were informed about take-off times, flight paths, likely weather conditions, the probable opposition, and so on, but each navigator was responsible for checking bearings and wind strengths during the flight so that he could advise his pilot to change course if necessary. The observer drew to scale on his chart a 'triangle of velocities' showing the aircraft's intended course, and another line indicating the course to be taken after allowing for wind direction and strength. This kind of navigation was called 'deduced reckoning', more familiarly known as 'dead reckoning'. However, if the calculations were less than accurate, over long distances the final error could be huge, possibly a matter of 50 miles or so from the intended target. Observers were trained in astro-navigation as well, but measuring the angle of a star and using a table to work out the position with reference to the ground below was not the easiest of tasks when sitting in a cold, cramped space and travelling at about 200 mph. Of course, on cloudy nights, astro-navigation was of limited use to the observer! To add to the crews' difficulties, the Blenheim was fitted with the same unreliable bombsight that older bombers had. Some cynical statisticians claimed that, in 1940, Bomber Command crews suffered more fatalities than the Germans being bombed by them. So it was that on the night of 25 August, over a hundred bombers flew to Berlin, but most of the bombs fell on the countryside to the south of the city causing civilian casualties, but little damage to vital industries. The Germans immediately planned vengeance.

At the Sportpalast in Berlin, on 4 September, Hitler threatened in his usual ranting style that if the British Air Force dropped 2000, 3000 or 4000 kilos of bombs, the *Luftwaffe* would respond a hundredfold in one night. If the RAF mounted large-scale attacks on German cities, then British cities would be eradicated. On Saturday 7 September, Tommy and his friends were at the 'Samson and Hercules' when it was announced that all Service personnel had to report to their units immediately. In local cinemas, similar instructions were flashed on to the screens. Tommy understood this to be an 'invasion imminent' alert. Back at RAF Watton, the Blenheims were bombed-up, with their engines running ready for action. Observers and gunners waited in the crew-room in full flying kit. The pilots sat in their cockpits prepared for take-off if reports came in that invasion barges were approaching the Lincolnshire beaches, but nothing happened, that is, until the 350 bomber attack on London started. The city suffered, but by changing their plan to destroy airfields and radar stations to wreaking their anger on Londoners, the Germans gave Fighter Command time to recover and regroup, so that a week later when another massive daylight raid on the capital occurred, the Hurricanes and Spitfires were waiting, and they shot down fifty-six German bombers.

Such a massive loss could not be sustained, so the *Luftwaffe* drastically reduced its daylight operations. In the last week of September, Berlin was bombed again. It was followed by seventy-six nights of continuous battering of London and other British cities. This onslaught from September 1940 until the middle of May 1941 (the *Luftwaffe's* farewell to London was on 10 May) caused the death of 40,000 civilians and made another 100,000 homeless. The

German High Command was certain that Britain would now sue for peace or, indeed, would surrender abjectly. But as was often heard said in the blitzed streets of the land, 'You can get used to anything'.

In utter frustration, the Germans had to abandon their invasion plans. It was the first battle that Hitler had failed to win, and for the British people it was a significant event especially in a psychological sense. A message was sent to the rest of the world, particularly America, that Britain could 'take it', and that any help given would not be wasted. Even so, in October 1940, Churchill warned (after a month of bombing), 'Death and sorrow will be the companions of our journey, hardship our garment, constancy and valour our only shield.' How could anyone fail to respond to such a glorious challenge?

Whilst all this was happening, Tommy was busy over the Channel ports. Ostend was the target on the night of 18 September. His crew went in at a height of 1500 feet, just low enough to be affected by the blast of a huge explosion in the dock below. The Blenheim was turned over on its back but Costello-Bowen, with superb skill, regained control. On 24 September, Calais harbour was bombed from 8000 feet. After that Costello-Bowen and Tommy did some 'abandoning by parachute' and 'dinghy' drills, a fortunate exercise in view of what happened two months later. On 4 October, there was a daylight raid on Hellevoetsluit harbour in Holland, where they encountered little trouble. Then they reverted to night operations, and bombed the barges at Dunkirk and Boulogne.

During October, 105 Squadron moved from Watton to Swanton Morley, also in Norfolk. On 25 October a raid on Osnabruck had to be abandoned because of fierce weather. Three days later, they were in the air for five hours on a bombing trip to Mannheim, flying over 700 miles into enemy territory. In November, they patrolled the aerodrome at Chartres and the one at Chateaudun some miles away, with the intention of making a nuisance of themselves by bombing and machine-gunning aircraft whenever they appeared on the flare-lit runway ready for take-off or having just landed. This was, probably, the first intruder raid of the war on an enemy aerodrome. They, in turn, were attacked by three fighters, but came to no harm. This sortie was followed by a similar one to Antwerp and Brussels the next night.

The Squadron suffered quite a few losses during these operations in the autumn of 1940, but Tommy's luck held out until the night of 26 November when the Squadron received orders to bomb the railway yards at Cologne, a strongly defended city. They reached the target and released the Blenheim's bomb load (4 x 250-pounders) just before they were hit by flak. Bad weather had been forecast for the return flight and it turned out to be really foul. Swanton Morley was covered in thick, low cloud, so there was no chance of landing there. Previously, they had been advised to make for RAF Valley in Anglesey in case of trouble, but by the time they reached the Midlands, they were running out of fuel and the bitter cold was causing the windscreen to ice up. Costello-Bowen circled round a few times, not only to use up the remaining fuel, but in the hope that down below a searchlight would be switched on to point the way to the nearest airfield, as was usually done to help aircraft in distress. By now, they were over the Pennine region of the Peak district. The cloud broke briefly, but all they could glimpse below was barren moorland rising to about 2000 feet. They climbed back into thick cloud and Costello-Bowen gave the order to abandon the Blenheim.

Sergeant Cameron, the air-gunner, went first (Sergeant Evans was off sick) followed by Tommy who went head first through the hatch. After a couple of seconds in the air, he pulled the ring on the rip-cord and the parachute opened. He could not see a thing in the cloud but, suddenly, a gap appeared just before he landed quite softly and safely on 'terra firma'. He saw a reddish glow in the distance, from where he assumed the aircraft had crashed and caught fire, which was to be expected, really, for the Blenheim had no self-sealing fuel tanks. He could see close by, framed by the glow, the outline of a building. It was well past midnight when he banged on the farmhouse door, and it took a while before the farmer came to the door with a shotgun in his hand pointing at Tommy! As soon as it was clear that it was not a German parachutist standing there, Tommy was invited in to have a warming cup of tea.

After meeting up again with his fellow crewmen, they telephoned 105 Squadron at Swanton Morley to report that they were safe but minus an aircraft. They were told that the Squadron had lost two other Blenheims that night. The three friends returned to the farmhouse to spend the rest of the night dozing in relative comfort, and in the morning they tucked into a splendid farmhouse breakfast. Later, an officer from RAF Ringway collected them and, all together, they went to examine the wreckage of the burnt-out Blenheim at the foot of the Pennines. It was a relief to Tommy to find out that he had managed to avoid a high-tension electricity cable barely 20 yards away from where he had landed. There was no doubt that Lady Luck was still smiling on him. Locally, the incident is recalled as the 'Harrop Edge Blenheim Crash'. The three of them stayed at RAF Ringway for a few days until everything was sorted out. They were billeted with a nice family at Wythenshawe – and were thoroughly spoilt, for each night they were taken to the local inn and treated to many a pint of beer by the pub's regular patrons. It is important to remember that, in those days especially, men were far more valuable than machines. There was a serious shortage of aircrew and airmen were taught, 'When in doubt, jump out.' The lives of bomber crews were particularly precious, for they were, then, the only men in Britain who could hit back at the Germans, so that in pubs and clubs all over Britain, their contribution to the war effort was readily appreciated in the usual pub way!

As soon as they returned to RAF Swanton Morley, they were medically examined, found fit, and given a fortnight's leave. In her diary, Mrs Broom wrote matter-of-factly, 'Tom home for 14 days. Had to bale out when plane crashed.' At the end of his leave, Tommy was presented with the Caterpillar Club's gold badge in recognition of the parachute drop that had saved his life.

By now, Tommy was one of the most experienced crewmen in the Squadron. He had nearly 300 hours' flying time to his credit, including over fifty hours of night flying, and he had completed eighteen operations against the enemy. He was regarded, also, as a man who could be relied on to carry out unpleasant tasks with good grace. Though the practice was frowned on by the RAF, some aircrew arranged for their wives to lodge at a local inn or hotel. Whenever Tommy and his friends went to the pub for a pint or two, the wives would often join them for company. One day, Tommy was asked by the Squadron Adjutant (who was responsible for all administrative and non-flying matters) if he would go down-town to prepare one of the wives for the news that her husband had been reported missing in action for, of course, the telegram informing the airman's next-of-kin would be sent to his official home address. It was not at all a comfortable task to perform for, though such sad news was not exactly uncommon, the wife was but a charming young girl, hardly out of her teens and too immature to cope with bitter tragedy. After being asked to carry out a similar task for a second time, Tommy made up his mind that he would not fall in love and marry. He felt that it would be unfair to burden a wife with the stress of being tied to an airman constantly flying over enemy territory. The 1945 film, 'The Way to the Stars' perfectly pictures the situation in which so many servicemen found themselves during the war.

Towards the end of 1940, the time had come for Tommy to leave 105 Squadron. As an instructor, he would use his experience, richly varied as it was, to benefit aspiring young crewmen.

CHAPTER SEVEN

Bitten by Mosquitoes

No. 13 Operational Training Unit (OTU) was based at RAF Bicester near Oxford. With Costello-Bowen, Tommy was stationed there as an instructor from December 1940 until January 1942. Life was busy enough with up to three flying training sorties daily, altogether about five hours in the air, though on one day in April 1941 nearly eight hours were logged. Nevertheless, it was a comfortable alternative to flying Blenheims on bombing missions in German skies. In a letter home just before Christmas 1940, Tom said that he had finished with operational flying, and that training future observers was a steady job with no worries. This was a most comforting message to his parents who had never ceased to worry about his safety and welfare.

Most of the pilots and observers who attended the OTU had received their initial training in Canada on Tiger Moths and Airspeed Oxfords. At Bicester, they underwent more rigorous training to prepare for air warfare. Whereas pilots underwent dual flight training in Blenheims, the navigators and air-gunners started off in Avro Ansons carrying out set exercises over the countryside to the west of Oxford. The Anson, or 'Faithful Annie' as it was known, was a good-natured, highly reliable, lumbering aircraft. It was the first monoplane to be in regular use with the RAF.

Quite often, Tommy would be asked to bring a reserve instructor with him. This meant that once the pilot had taken off safely, he would hand over the controls to Tommy so that he could finish reading whichever book he was absorbed in at the time. Tommy delighted in this 'amateur' piloting and, of course, it was yet another useful experience for him. Perhaps it was fortunate, therefore, that the trusty old Anson had no vices!

After completing their training, pilots, navigators and air-gunners crewed up according to personal preference, after which they progressed to operational training in Blenheims. However, from June onwards, Tommy flew rather less and spent more time supervising, for example, checking log-sheets for the cross-country flights and, of course, giving valuable advice to the young airmen. If, however, there was low-level or formation flying, invariably Tommy would be required to accompany the leader. From Bicester, a typical route would take them to Stow-on-the-Wold, Craven Arms, Much Wenlock, Tewkesbury, Alcester and back to Bicester, a flight path over some of the most beautiful of Cotswold and Wenlock Edge villages. Tommy found the low-level flights particularly exhilarating, even though the navigation was tricky.

At Bicester, in the spring of 1941, Tommy came across another Broom. Ivor Broom was a fresh-faced young sergeant-pilot attending the six-week course before being posted to a Blenheim squadron. Their paths would cross again during the war, and again and again for over sixty years after that as well.

As an ex-armourer, Tommy was especially useful to the Flight. In addition, as part of his observer's course at Aldergrove before the war, he had already completed a bombing course, so that he was more knowledgeable than most about the technicalities of bombing. Despite all his experience, he was sent to RAF Manby on a Bombing Leader's course with the intention of keeping him at Bicester, which was really a waste of time and resources. More often than not, Tommy knew rather more than those instructing him did and, in any case, he had no wish to stay at Bicester.

Tommy's old 105 Squadron, stationed at RAF Swanton Morley once more, had suffered terrible losses during its service in Malta. When it returned to a home base, it needed to be recharged, and the boost came in the form of the Mosquito, three of which were delivered by Geoffrey de Havilland Jnr himself. One of the first pilots to fly a Mosquito was F/Lt George Parry, who had been at Bicester with Tommy. In fact, Tommy had been his navigator on quite a few occasions at the OTU and, together, they had led formations of three aircraft on low-level training flights. However, the grass airfield at RAF Swanton Morley was unsuitable so 105 Squadron was moved to RAF Horsham St Faith in December 1941. It was about this time that Tommy and Costello-Bowen were seriously considering the idea of returning to operational duties.

When they heard rumours that their old Squadron was being re-equipped with a new wonder bomber, they decided to do something about it. On a visit to Horsham St Faith, Costello-Bowen was promised by Wing Commander Peter Simmons, whom they both knew, that if they could sort things out at Bicester, they would be most welcome to rejoin the Squadron. At 13 OTU they had another ally in G/Capt Kyle, the Station Commander, and another old acquaintance.

Both Costello-Bowen and Tommy had enjoyed their time at Bicester. It was a very pleasant little town, just a mile or so from the airfield and easily accessible from there. Their favourite local was the 'Crown' whose landlady was the charming Mrs Tilt. The hotel had a cinema attached and, of greater significance perhaps, for the beer gave them a ravenous appetite, on the way back to the aerodrome from the 'Crown' there was a fish-and-chip shop. Monday was the most popular day off, for it was market day at Bicester and the pubs were open until nearly tea-time to refresh the visiting farmers.

Three of the airmen got together and decided to arrange a trip to London for a change. If you knew your way around there, and had an inkling of opening and closing times, you could do very well for yourself. By 6 o'clock they had reached the 'Criterion Restaurant' in Piccadilly Circus. They were undoubtedly a little inebriated by this time and noisily cheerful, so they were asked to move to a table on the other side of the room. They were offended by this rather superior attitude towards decent servicemen, so they refused to budge. A posse of Military Police was summoned and arrived promptly, accompanied by an officious Provost Marshal from the RAF. A minor scuffle broke out. All three were arrested and pushed into the back of a military vehicle. Tommy walked right through to the front of the van, stepped out and ran off. He was soon recaptured and they were put in the cells at the Guards' Barracks at Chelsea. The next morning, they were escorted back to Bicester and brought before the Station Commander. G/Capt Kyle understood that his men needed the occasional fling. He would do what he could for them. Some time later, they had to return to Chelsea for a Court of Inquiry where a summary of evidence was given and witnesses cross-examined. After a meal and a drink in the Mess, they were sent back to Bicester with the threat of a court martial hanging over them – quite a serious matter in the Forces. Three weeks later, G/Capt Kyle called them in and explained that since there was a critical shortage of aircrew, they would be severely reprimanded only. In fact, it was not long before Tommy was promoted to Flight Sergeant and soon after to Warrant Officer.

In February 1942, the same month that 'Bomber' Harris assumed command, Costello-Bowen (now a Pilot Officer) and Tommy rejoined 105 Squadron at RAF Horsham St Faith near Norwich. The station was equipped with six de Havilland Mosquitoes. Tommy's first flight in one (W4071) with Costello-Bowen was on 15 February. It lasted for ¾ hour. During his early days back with the squadron, Tommy flew in all the Mosquitoes, including W4066, the first to fly with Bomber Command (apart, that is, from the ones used by the Photo Reconnaissance Unit). Many flight tests had to be performed and several short specialist courses attended, including a few days spent training with the Army and the Royal Navy. By the time the two of them had made a 4½-hour trip to the Shetlands and back, had practised one-engine-only landings, found out about fuel consumption figures, gone on mock bombing runs, carried out some photographic work, learned Morse code and how to operate wireless sets, they were considered well-qualified to cope with crewing the two-seater Mosquito. Of course, to ensure adequate flying experience, they had to use other available aircraft as well – Blenheims, Ansons, Tiger Moths and Miles Masters. They particularly enjoyed the Tiger Moth for it was so manoeuvrable in the air and such fun to fly. At the end of this period, the Air Observers were regraded as Navigators (BW), the B standing for Bomb Aimer and the W for Wireless Operator.

By the end of May 1942, more Mosquitoes had been acquired and the Squadron was declared operational once more. The night of 30 May had seen the first 1000 bomber raid on Cologne. In daylight on the following morning, a Flight from Horsham St Faith carried out the first Mosquito operation of the war. The three aircraft took off separately, Wing Commander Oakshott at 0540 hours, P/O Kennard at 0740 hours and Costello-Bowen and Tommy at 1140 hours. They stoked up the fires that had been lit in Cologne with their 500-pound bombs, but could not photograph the devastation that had been wrought upon the city because of the clouds of smoke. On the return flight, P/O Kennard's plane was shot down over the Scheldt estuary, but the others got back safely.

There was another major operation on 25 June, which coincided with the 1000-bomber raid on Bremen. Costello-Bowen and Tommy had orders to attack the airfield at Schleswig-Jagel where Junkers 88 night-fighters were stationed. They reached their target as dusk was falling and bombed from a height of about 100 feet with good results. They could certainly claim to have made a low-level attack! The success of their raid ensured that there would be fewer night-fighters to harass the heavy bombers later on that night over Bremen. The trip lasted nearly 3½ hours altogether, so that by the time they returned to base, night had set in, but they still landed without mishap. Later on, there was some controversy concerning Mosquito landings at night. One senior officer claimed that he had been the first pilot to land a Mosquito in the dark – in 1943 – but, of course, Costello-Bowen and Tommy knew otherwise, for they had managed it a year earlier.

On 2 July, Costello-Bowen and Tommy (in DK295) were involved in another 'first', a daylight formation sortie at low-level. Their target was the submarine yard at Flensburg. Five Mosquitoes flew low over the North Sea, but their approach was forewarned by German fishing-boats, equipped with radio, sailing way out at sea. The British airmen called them 'squealers'. There was a hot reception waiting for them as they flew right into the harbour. Ship and shore guns put up a curtain of fire, but the crews kept together in formation to make sure that the target was not missed. Unfortunately, the leader, G/Capt Macdonald, crashed after being hit by flak. The pilots had been instructed to split up after the attack, and to return to base along a flight path that would take them near to the Fresian Islands. Costello-Bowen and Tommy regarded the plan ill thought, so they agreed to fly towards the middle stretches of the North Sea instead. German fighters were swarming around, and they shot down the Mosquito piloted by W/Cdr Oakshott. During the flight, Tommy had to keep a wary eye open so that he could warn Costello-Bowen to take evasive action if there was any threat to their safety, for the Mosquito bomber was unarmed and could not take part in any dogfights. The three remaining

Mosquitoes landed safely despite the frantic chase. It was fortunate that their 'Wooden Wonders' could outpace the fastest of the German fighters at that time. Though they mourned the loss of their comrades, the experiences of war had hardened them into a fatalistic kind of thinking quite common in airmen constantly in danger. They tended to express their feelings off-handedly with the almost callous, 'That's life.' They hardly ever considered the possibility that such a fate could be theirs or, at least, that was the impression they continued to give in public. On the very next day, Costello-Bowen took Tommy to Bristol (Whitchurch) in a Bisley, the latest variant of the Blenheim, to start a well-earned leave.

The two of them were back in action on 16 July. They were supposed to make a low-level attack at Vegesack. Because of thick cloud, they were unable to locate the target, so they sought an alternative one, but for some reason the bomb-release mechanism would not function. Dame Fortune smiled on them again as they flew in and landed at Horsham St Faith without any bother. This was followed by another unsuccessful sortie. As they were on their way to Münster, the intercom failed. To continue the mission without being able to communicate with each other would have been to court danger foolishly, so the trip was aborted.

Towards the end of the month, the two of them took a Mosquito to Gransden Lodge, a highly secret radar-testing station. A system known as Gee had been introduced following its development by a research establishment based at Worth Matravers. Lattice lines that had been drawn on charts needed to be checked for accuracy. Tommy's place was often taken by an RAF 'boffin' (scientist). The Mosquito was flown towards targets along the lattice lines. Photographs were taken during the flight, which were checked to make sure that the chart markings corresponded with the actual path taken by the aircraft. During this period of comparative inactivity, Tommy kept himself busy by picking up enough information about Gee to make himself a quite competent operator. He became so proficient, in fact, that he was asked to act as an instructor to some naval officers who were being trained in a Vickers Wellington bomber[10]. It was at this time, when he was comfortably safe in a secret location, that Tommy had the narrowest possible escape from disaster. There was no Flying Control at Gransden

Lodge, so that when the Wellington that Tommy was in took off, another Wellington was rushing down a second runway that crossed its path. Tommy was in the astro-hatch and could see what was going to happen. Just before the intersection, in answer to Tommy's prayer, his pilot, P/O Wilmot, managed to get just enough lift to scrape over the other Wellington. But to Tommy with his grandstand view, it had all been too close for comfort.

At about the same time, there was a second incident that was more amusing than life-threatening, though some of the participants may have thought otherwise. On one of the Wellington training flights, the pilot left the cockpit and stepped casually to the rear of the plane to have a chat with the trainees. One of the naval officers was so horrified at this apparent madness and dereliction of duty of care, that he dashed to the cockpit to take over to save them all from a dreadful end. Of course, he found Tommy contentedly and confidently piloting the craft. During his time at Horsham St Faith, Tommy had done quite a bit of casual piloting under supervision, concentrating on take-off and landing procedures in trainers (usually the Tiger Moth), and he had been at the controls of an Avro Anson earlier in his career. What had seemed a potentially horrifying situation to the naval officer, turned out to be but a topic of teasing hilarity in the Mess afterwards.

In August, back once more at Horsham St Faith, the Duke of Kent was due to make a visit. Costello-Bowen and Tommy had taken off at daybreak on a high-level raid on the Krupp factories at Essen. The weather conditions were perfect for making contrails (condensed vapour trails) as they crossed the North Sea. The ploy then was to lose height until the trails disappeared. Any contrails above them now would signal the presence of German fighters. They reached their target, bombed the plant and photographed the damage before hastily making tracks for home. Very soon, they spotted contrails above them, so they dived into a layer of cloud at about 8000 feet. They had a peep out now and again, but there were two Messerschmitt 109s not far away and seemingly always present, so back into the cloud they went. Over the Scheldt estuary, the cloud was breaking up, so they dived to sea level, just missing a Junkers 88 returning to Holland. Costello-Bowen and Tommy were told later that they had been plotted on radar (for the benefit of the

Duke) and that shadowing them had been two squadrons of fighters (eighteen in all) out for the kill. It was no wonder that whenever they broke cloud, they always saw Messerschmitts! Clearly, the Germans did not like the idea of Krupp's plant (so crucial to their war needs) being bombed in daylight by these cheeky Britishers. When they landed, the Duke of Kent was in the operations room, waiting to hear their story in greater detail. Sadly a month later the Duke was killed in an air-crash. He was on active service as Chief Welfare Officer of RAF Home Command when the Sunderland flying-boat, on its way to Iceland, crashed in the north of Scotland. Though Tommy himself seemed to be leading a charmed life with 'Doom' passing him by, very soon he would have to think rather more seriously about what the consequences might be of leading such a chancy kind of life.

When Tommy transferred from the Blenheim to a Mosquito, it seemed as if he had moved from a 'steady old Rover' to a 'hotted-up Rolls-Royce'. 'Hotted-up' was an apt adjective for, unlike the freezing interiors of Blenheims, Ansons and Oxfords, the Mosquito had a heated cockpit. In the bitter winter of 1940, Blenheim aircrews were warned not to handle instruments without gloves on in case their hands became frozen to the metal. Further, whereas the Bristol-engined Blenheim was capable of 250 mph, the Rolls-Royce Merlin-powered Mosquito could reach speeds approaching 400 mph. Though it was a light bomber with two crewmen on board, it had the manoeuvrability of a fighter, could operate at high altitudes and even climb smoothly with only one engine working. Best of all, perhaps, it could outpace all the existing German fighters. Whereas the Battles, Hampdens, Whitleys and Blenheims, and even Wellingtons, had been described as museum pieces, the arrival of the Mosquito brought about a change of attitude amongst bomber crews – there was now more than pride and hope, there was a knowledge of certain success. Before the war, the Air Ministry had planned to build heavily armed bombers of metal construction, but implementation of the policy was delayed so that the first of the four-engined bombers did not appear on the scene until February 1941. The Short Stirling was not entirely successful. In strong cross-winds it veered dangerously off course, and it could not climb high enough to avoid being hit by flak. Months later, when the vastly better Avro Lancasters and Handley-Page Halifaxes came on the scene and flew from 10,000 to 20,000 feet higher up, their high-explosive and incendiary bombs rained down on the Stirlings below. Understandably, the Stirlings were taken out of service!

When de Havilland offered to develop a fast light-bomber in 1938, the Air Ministry showed no real interest, but when the successful U-boat campaign caused a severe shortage of metal-alloys, it was eventually forced to consider aircraft of wooden construction. When the Mosquito did appear, it was christened 'Freeman's Folly', a tribute to Air Marshal Freeman who had authorised de Havilland to proceed with design work for a bomber with a range of 1500 miles and capable of carrying a 1000-pound bomb load – a foolish fancy! Fifty were ordered in March 1940, but when France capitulated, understandably, priority was given to the production of already proven aircraft, in particular, Hurricane and Spitfire fighters and Blenheim and Wellington bombers.

By November 1940, less than a year after design work had started, a Mosquito was flown for half-an-hour. Within another year, test flights and reconnaissance trips across the Channel had been completed, and the RAF had been equipped with the first dozen Mosquitoes, half of them to 105 Squadron at Swanton Morley. To the men who flew it, and the men who serviced it, the Mosquito was a 'Wooden Wonder'. Its wings, tail and fuselage were made of laminated timber held together by strong adhesives though, according to Alf Harrington, one of Tommy's village friends, it had, also, 3000 brass screws that were turned out at Mustad's nail-factory in Portishead – a nice coincidence for Tommy. Another unusual feature of the Mosquito bomber was that it was unarmed, so could not afford to take part in any direct confrontation with enemy fighters. Instead, it had to avoid battle by flying fast and high, or fast and low, to keep out of trouble. Fortunately, the Mosquito easily exceeded the Air Ministry's requirements; its range was about right; its bomb load was either 2000 pounds (4 x 500) or 4000 pounds (the 'cookie', a blast-bomb drum filled with molten explosive – and four times a Blenheim's bomb load); it could travel at 400 mph and it could climb to a ceiling of 30,000 feet, at which height the damp air inside the aircraft would condense on the surface of the cold Perspex windows and freeze, covering them with a fine film of ice. This problem was solved in later versions, and the Mosquito could fly higher and, equipped with Merlin 61 engines, was the fastest aircraft in the world. Armed with 4 x 20-mm cannon and 4 x .303-machine-guns, the Mosquito packed a formidable punch indeed. The liquid-cooled Rolls-Royce Merlins were such superb engines that when four of them were fitted to the accident-prone Avro Manchester, the brilliant Lancaster was born.

The 'Wooden Wonder' was far more important than just for its ability to carry out spectacular raids, though they were most welcome in those dark days of 1942. Logistically, the Mosquito surpassed all other bombers. The slow Blenheim with its 4 x 250-pound bomb load could not stand comparison. Even the renowned Avro Lancaster could not match the Mosquito. Certainly, it could carry four or five times the load, but it cost three times more to build, and required seven crewmen to fly it and, since it was more vulnerable to fighter attack and flak, its casualty rate was easily ten times that of the Mosquito. In addition, the Mosquito could pinpoint targets and attack them at low-level. Taking everything into consideration, the Mosquito was arguably the finest aircraft in the history of wartime flying.

When Costello-Bowen and Tommy flew a Mosquito to Cologne in May 1942, it was as part of the first Mosquito operation against an enemy target. By this time, of course, the Squadron had moved to Horsham St Faith. Nos 105 and 139 Squadrons caused considerable embarrassment to the Germans who had, hitherto, scorned the capacity of the RAF to achieve anything at all striking. However, when, for example, 105 Squadron made a low-level attack on the *Gestapo* Headquarters in Oslo, it became obvious that even individual buildings in European cities could be specifically targeted and destroyed. In January 1943, the same squadron made the first Mosquito attack on Berlin, ruining a parade organised for the benefit of Hermann Goering, the *Luftwaffe's* leader and Hitler's senior deputy. It was especially pleasing to humiliate him, for it was Goering who had boasted some years earlier that the RAF would never get through to bomb the German capital. Similarly, 139 Squadron scattered a parade gathered to listen to one of Dr Goebbels's tirades. These isolated events were signals of what would follow later. As Sir Arthur Harris had predicted, the Germans would reap the whirlwind after sowing the wind.

CHAPTER EIGHT

A Little Trip Abroad

W/Cdr Hughie Edwards VC, DFC took over command of 105 Squadron at Horsham St Faith on 3 August 1942. The heroic Australian had won the country's greatest honour when he had led a Blenheim squadron in a raid on Bremen in July 1941. It seems that they flew so low that they went under the high-tension cables that fringed the target! Within a week of this change of command, Tom wrote home, 'I have good news for you – will be home on leave again on August the 25th – that is, will be home the evening before.' However, Fate determined otherwise.

On that very day, three crews were detailed to raid two power stations at Cologne and a switching-station at Brauweiler nearby. Costello-Bowen and Tommy were in distinguished company. The other Mosquitoes were crewed by George Parry and George (Robbie) Robson (of Oslo fame), and Roy Ralston and Sydney Clayton. Roy was possibly the finest of all low-level attack pilots in the RAF and, later on, proved to be an extremely popular Commanding Officer.

They took off at 7.15 p.m. and flew in formation to the mouth of the Scheldt, where they split up to make their separate ways. Costello-Bowen and Tommy, in DK297, flew so low after crossing the coast that they sometimes brushed the tops of trees. After hopping over one small wood, an electricity pylon barred their way. Costello-Bowen pulled up to avoid it, but the starboard engine struck the pylon at its very top. Immediately, both the engine and its propeller stopped, and the controls became completely jammed.

They were moving at about 250 mph just 80 feet above ground. There was absolutely nothing they could do to avoid disaster. They could only wait for the Mosquito to crash into the fields below. Tommy called out to Costello-Bowen, 'Well this is it.' Yet though death was imminent, neither of them seemed worried. They kept surprisingly calm.

Some twenty or thirty seconds after hitting the pylon and crossing a few fields, a pine wood loomed in front of them. A violent, head-on crash was unavoidable. Just before they hit the trees, Tommy instinctively released his safety belt. To this day he does not know why he did it. They crashed and, for Tommy, everything went black. He did not feel any physical pain, he just sensed complete darkness and felt himself rolling over and over like a powered ball. He must have been flung out of the plane through the cockpit cover, but how it happened he could not fathom. Though it did not seem so at the time, Tommy must have been unconscious for quite a while, possibly as long as half-an-hour. When he came to, covered in branches and bits of aeroplane, a strong smell of petrol was in the air. Yet, amazingly, the wooden Mosquito had not caught fire. Neither had the bombs exploded. The only possible explanation was that the nose of the aircraft must have squeezed through between two trees!

Tommy realised that he had not suffered any substantial injury, not even a scratch as far as he could see. His next thought was for Costello-Bowen's fate. It was nearly dark by now, but Tommy found him lying in some wreckage not far away, unconscious and in poor shape. His shoes had been torn off, presumably by the rudder pedals. Tommy patted Costello-Bowen's face and talked to him urgently in order to elicit some response. After a while, he muttered one or two words shakily. Then, when he was more or less awake, Tommy lifted him up gently and carried him to a sheltered spot some hundred yards away. There they rested to give themselves time to recover from the shock, but they were soon chatting and speculating about their immediate situation. The thought of imprisonment made them somewhat despondent. However, they were in isolated countryside and it would be some time before anyone, whether German or local, found them. Costello-Bowen's ankle was extremely painful and, though he had made a partial recovery, he was still in shock. Tommy himself felt reasonably comfortable considering all that had happened, but he was 'browned-off' to think that his great adventure had come to an end.

After a further brief discussion, they decided to move away from the scene of the crash and to attempt making contact with an escape organisation. Apart from the fact that spending the rest of the war as prisoners-of-war did not appeal to them, they knew that it was their duty as airmen to avoid capture if at all possible. Costello-Bowen voiced doubts about his ability to cope and, after giving the matter serious consideration, he suggested that Tommy should go it alone. Tommy agreed, but his heart got the better of his brain and, after just a few hesitant steps, back he went to tend to his comrade's needs. They had emergency rations, which included Benzedrine tablets, so they had one each to ease their depression. With Costello-Bowen leaning on and clinging to him, Tommy led the way. They had just reached a country lane when they heard someone approaching. Instantly, they dived behind a hedge, and the traveller passed by without noticing them. By this time it was getting quite dark, but they set off determinedly across the fields and steadily made headway. Costello-Bowen seemed to be recovering well now and, feeling much better, began to walk without Tommy's support.

It was essential for them to find a hiding place before dawn. There would be little chance of escape if they were seen in open countryside during daylight. Eventually they came to a small wood, no more than a hundred yards' square, with conifers of Christmas tree-size growing in it. They settled down and even managed to doze for a while. They were wakened by a church clock striking in the distance. Feeling very thirsty, they walked along the edge of the wood to see if there was a small stream nearby. They found a muddy ditch instead. Its stagnant water did not look at all inviting, but they had rubber bags and purifying tablets in their emergency packs that enabled them to produce a liquid that was good enough to refresh them despite its provenance and doubtful vintage. They continued their search, keeping just inside the edge of the wood to avoid being seen. After a while, they spotted what seemed to be a hutted camp. They lay low, hidden from the various tracks that criss-crossed the wood, but able to keep the camp under observation.

There were no guards at the entrance gate. During the four hours or so that they kept watch, they saw no German soldiers, only nurses going to and fro. They assumed that it must be some kind of field hospital, so they decided to take a chance. They knew that the Germans would be looking for them where they had crashed, but they were not sure how far they had managed to scramble their way during the night. In any case, surely they would have seen some soldiers if there had been any stationed at the camp. They walked over and knocked at the first hut, which they guessed was an office of some kind. A nurse came to the door. She was startled to see these bedraggled-looking men in RAF uniform, but she recognised them for what they were and went inside to fetch a doctor who could speak English. He said that he had heard about the plane crash and he knew that the Germans were searching for them, but he assured Tommy and Costello-Bowen that he would do what he could for them. They said that they wished to get in touch with the people in charge of the escape-line for British airmen, and that the only way they could do this would be if they could visit the cafes and restaurants near the railway station in Antwerp. The doctor was most anxious to help and promised that he would get in touch with his friends in the town who might be able to give him precise information. Tommy and Costello-Bowen were given a boiled egg each and a hot drink. It was arranged that they would return to their hiding place. Each evening at 6 o'clock, an English-speaking nurse would pass by the edge of the wood and whistle a few bars of a current, well-known tune. This would be the signal for Tommy to approach to collect a bottle of drinking water and a tomato sandwich each, and to receive any fresh news.

The skies were cloudless. During the sweltering day, the two of them became dry and parched, but at night they froze in the clear, cold air. However, in their escape kits, they had Horlicks tablets, barley sugar and some chocolate bars to sustain them, as well as a compass and a mini-razor. Tommy had a thick pullover that he wore for half the night before handing it over to Costello. They had, also, a large silk handkerchief on which was printed a map of Germany and surrounding areas. The days dragged. They often heard German soldiers marching along the road, but they avoided detection.

Though their predicament only lasted from Wednesday to Friday, it seemed as if weeks had gone by. On that last day, they were told that no contact had been made and that they would have to move on. It was explained that if they were caught in the wood, the local inhabitants would be accused of harbouring them and that reprisals would follow. As soon as darkness fell, Tommy and Costello-Bowen moved off, but had only covered a short distance when the nurse caught up with them and reported that all was well. At 6 o'clock on Saturday, someone would come along to start them on their way. Oddly, neither of them felt elated. They seemed to take everything for granted, as if life's unexpected occurrences were ordained to fall into place. All that would change, and very soon.

They both slept soundly on that Friday night and, though Saturday dragged along as if it would never end, in time they heard with relief the nurse's familiar whistle. She was accompanied by another young woman who received an equally warm welcome from Tommy and Costello-Bowen. Before leaving, they told the nurse that all they could do was to thank her and her colleagues for all the risks they had taken, and that their courage and kindness would never be forgotten. If the nurses and doctors had been suspected of aiding the two airmen, their lives would surely have been forfeited.

With their new companion, Tommy and Costello-Bowen returned to their den in the wood. There, the girl questioned them in detail to establish that the two of them were bona-fide British airmen and not German secret agents. It seemed that she already knew their names, home addresses, their squadron numbers and their Station Commander's name. She, or her compatriots, had clearly been in touch with the British authorities by radio, so that she was able to ask pertinent questions to check their identity. She did not offer to tell them her name. As she explained, the less they knew the safer it was for everybody, for if one of them were captured and tortured, a name might be revealed and a chain reaction started that might implicate everyone involved in the organisation. She had a suitcase with her that contained suits, shirts and ties, bottles of water, a lather brush, razors and a towel. They washed, shaved and changed, then they buried their uniforms out of sight of prying eyes. They were given a small attaché case each, with a few items included in them. She said that she was going to take them down the road. They would have a drink in the village cafe and wait there until it was time to catch the tram for Antwerp, which was only about 20 miles away. She emphasised that she would do all the talking that was necessary. Tommy asked if there were any German soldiers in the village. She replied that there would be numerous encounters, but they were to behave exactly as they would if they were visiting for the first time an English town where they were strangers. Tommy was afraid that he would be nervous or embarrassed and, perhaps, let them down, at which she responded nonchalantly, 'You'll get used to it!'

Away they went to have a beer at the cafe. There were German soldiers walking about the village. To Tommy's relief, he felt quite comfortable in their presence. In time, they boarded a tram. There was no room to sit down, so they stood in the corridor. Just before reaching Antwerp, the tram came to a sudden halt. Local police and Germans in uniform came on board looking for black-marketeers. It was as well that identity cards were not examined for the two airmen had none. When they alighted at Antwerp, Tommy and Costello-Bowen followed the girl discreetly to a doctor's house, where she left them until the following day, which was a Sunday. The doctor was most hospitable. After they had had a cold bath, they were given a boiled egg with slices of bread, just a little meal to get their stomachs accustomed to proper food once more. After the snack, they sat chatting, had a beer, then retired thankfully to bed.

Meantime, at Rhondda Villas, Mrs Broom recorded in her diary on 26 August that a telegram had been received from the Air Ministry informing her that Tom was missing in action. She added with gratitude that Bob and Peter had come home to comfort her. In the following month, Mrs Broom received numerous letters of condolence. Many of them expressed the hope that Tom was safe as a prisoner-of-war in German hands. This would be the lesser of two evils, so the wish was kindly meant. Of course, though they had known Tom for many years, they had little measure of his spirit or resourcefulness. Neither had they any knowledge of the courage so readily shown by his Belgian and French rescuers. The RAF recorded the event differently. In a Personnel Occurrence Report under the sub-heading of Postings, it was noted that W/O T.J. Broom of No. 105 Squadron at Horsham St Faith had been posted to No. 1 RAF Depot (Missing) with effect from 25.8.42. This statistic (just one of tens of thousands) could not possibly be expected to reflect the anguish felt by his family and friends. Even so, when read half a century later, it does seem a cold, detached reference to a potentially tragic happening.

In Antwerp, plans were being effected to secure Tommy and Costello-Bowen's safety. After breakfast, their young guide called for them and led them to the station to catch a train leaving for Brussels. They arrived in the Belgian capital and were promptly taken to a house a short walk away. They were made most welcome by a grand, elderly lady who lived alone. She assured the two of them that they would be quite safe with her, for she had been raided by the Germans the previous week when they had scoured the street for anyone they suspected of having committed a misdemeanour against the occupying forces, or were deemed to be undesirable because of their apparent Jewishness no matter how innocent their conduct. At her home, Tommy and Costello had their first taste of black, doughy bread, dandelion salad and horse-meat!

Late on Monday afternoon, they were collected and guided to the 'Bon Marché' store to have their identity photographs taken. As soon as they got inside, a German put his hand on Tommy's shoulder and muttered some words that Tommy could not understand. Then he turned away without waiting for a response. The guide hurried to Tommy's side and whispered that the instruction had been to leave the store as it was closing time. To Tommy, it seemed strange that he had reacted more with surprise than fear at this encounter, a sign that he was getting used to things, as his guide had predicted. On Tuesday, they tried once more to obtain the necessary photographs, and this time they were successful. Then, they were moved to another safe house in readiness for a crucial part of their adventure. They stayed with Carl Servai's family for the rest of the day. (Of course, Tommy did not find out his real name until the end of 1944, when he received a joyful card from Carl in the newly liberated city of Brussels.) Tommy and Costello-Bowen made a fuss of Carl's little daughter whom they christened 'Chumleigh'. At Carl's house, they were introduced to the guide who would take care of them on the journey to Paris. (Tommy found out, in 1962, that the guide's name was Albert Johnson.) He presented them with false identity cards and he promised to pick them up for the trip early the next morning. In a way, they were sorry to leave such a delightful home.

Pierre (Tommy's assumed name) and his friend were given a

picture magazine each by Albert Johnson. They were told to follow him on to the train, to find a seat as near to him as possible, and to immerse themselves in the magazines so that other passengers would not wish to interrupt their reading. The carriage had an open, central passageway with cubicle-style seating on both sides. There were four seats in each bay, with two sets of two facing each other. Tommy and Costello-Bowen obeyed their instructions faithfully. On examining the tickets they had been given, they discovered that they were bound for Lille, not Paris as they had assumed. The thinking behind this was that the Germans would expect evading airmen to head as quickly as possible for the capital to lose themselves in the busy, crowded city. On the train, Costello-Bowen secured a seat by Albert's side, whereas Tommy had to sit further away next to a Belgian soldier in a black uniform. Very soon after leaving Brussels, German police and *Gestapo* agents entered the carriage and demanded that all passengers should be ready to show their official papers. They examined Albert's and Costello-Bowen's identity cards, and returned them without comment. However, they were not satisfied with the Belgian soldier's documents and he was marched off under escort.

Now it was Tommy's turn. He felt apprehensive after seeing the Belgian's dismissive treatment. He handed over his identity card. Something was said that Tommy could not understand, but as a gesture of co-operation he handed over his train ticket. Another question was asked. Since he had nothing else to hand over, Tommy just muttered, 'Hmm', hoping that it would suffice. Apparently the mumbled answer was quite adequate for all his papers were handed back without further ado. Albert had heard this cross-examination but, of course, had not interfered as such an action would only have created suspicion. When the Germans were out of earshot, Albert explained quietly that the first question had been, 'Where are you going?' Handing over the ticket had provided a perfectly appropriate answer. The second question had been whether Pierre was on his way to work at the mines near Lille, and Tommy's 'Hmm' had been taken as an affirmation.

The train was stopped at the frontier post between Belgium and France, where all the passengers had to alight to report to the check-point with their belongings. There was nothing in Tommy's or Costello-Bowen 's attaché cases to arouse suspicion. From the frontier tc Lille, the journey was uninterrupted and comfortable. They dined at a restaurant not far from the station, walked round to stretch their legs, then returned to the station to board a train for Paris. No further checks were made on the train, neither was there any trouble at the Gare du Nord. The three of them walked to a safe house, where their loyal guide left them.

The flat's owner was a jovial kind of person, and he looked after Tommy and Costello-Bowen (as well as two other evaders) with much kindness. He told them, with some glee in his voice, that once they had departed, he would have a 'holiday'. During his off-duty hours, he would act as host to a group of German officers whom he would entertain royally. It was from the Germans that he obtained such quantities of high quality food with which to feast his present guests. What a rogue, and what a man of courage! He turned over one of the family portraits hanging on the wall to disclose a picture of Adolf Hitler in all his glory and, quite naturally, this would be the one on display when his German guests were being entertained. In fact, he could claim to be one of the Germans' favourite Frenchmen, but it was a dangerous game that he played. If he were found out, his punishment would be merciless.

When Tommy and Costello-Bowen ventured outside the flat, they had to be exceptionally careful. Not only had they to be wary of being overheard conversing in English, but also they had to avoid smoking English cigarettes. Continental people would too easily identify their distinctive aroma. Though Tommy managed to get hold of some coarse French tobacco, he did not smoke it in public for not many Frenchmen seemed to enjoy pipe-smoking, and Tommy did not want to do anything that would jeopardise their safety.

On Saturday, they were taken to another safe house. There they met the man who would supply the documents permitting them to travel through the normally forbidden zone along the Atlantic coast, which the Germans had occupied as far south as the Spanish border. In fact, he was writing and stamping their passes just then! In later years, Tommy found out that the man was Frederic (Freddy) de Jongh who, with his daughter Dedee[11], bravely led the 'Comete' escape organisation.

On receiving their fresh documents, Tommy and Costello-Bowen handed over their emergency money-packages, which contained French, Belgian and Dutch notes. Then, after considerable discussion, it was agreed that Costello-Bowen should stay on in Paris to give him time to recover properly from his minor, but troublesome, injuries. Tommy learned later that Costello-Bowen really enjoyed his extra week's rest. He spent much of his time out and about, walking with purpose to recover his fitness and to build up his stamina for what was to come. He must have been fairly relaxed, for he had the nerve to visit a cinema one evening. On the Sunday that they parted company, Tommy had to make contact with a fresh guide. He left the house with an hour and a half to spare before he was due to report to the Gare d'Austerlitz at 10 o'clock that night. He was told to turn left when he was outside the front door and to walk a hundred yards or so along the street until he came to a jeweller's shop. There he would see a girl in a red hat examining the contents of the window. She was the guide who would look after him on the Metro. They met, greeted each other, and went on their way.

In the compartment, they were surrounded by Germans in uniform. Two of them sat on the seat opposite. After a while, one of them leaned forward and said something to Tommy. Quick as a flash, his 'girlfriend' butted in and answered, then she nudged Tommy and indicated that the two of them should leave. She did not want to give the soldier time to ponder why Tommy had not deigned to answer his query. Neither did she want to give him an opportunity to start a casual conversation with them. They got off the Metro and walked the rest of the way.

When they reached the Gare d'Austerlitz, the young girl in the red hat disappeared as soon as she had handed Tommy over to Frederic de Jongh, who was waiting on the platform in the company of Albert Johnson, another girl and three more evaders, one of them a Polish airman. (They were 'evaders' rather than 'escapers' for the simple reason that they had not been caught yet!) They all possessed the requisite documents (tickets, identity cards and Atlantic Coast passes) to let them through and so they boarded the train for St Jean de Luz.

Freddy de Jongh was a fantastic hero. He had reserved a

compartment for them all, but when they reached it, they found it already occupied by people who were not prepared to vacate their precious seats. Without hesitation, Freddy fetched the German train-commander and other officials to sort out the problem. The intruders were ordered out so that Freddy and his travelling companions could enjoy their journey in comfort, and a most pleasant trip it turned out to be. Though their papers were checked, nothing was found amiss and, when the train-commander came round later to ensure that all was well, and to wish them a happy and trouble-free night's journey, they were truly charmed as well as highly amused.

They reached St Jean de Luz at 7 o'clock in the morning. There was a tricky situation to be faced when they disembarked. All the passengers queued as they exited through the one door that had been made available. On each side of the door, there were German and French officials checking travel warrants and identity papers. They tended to stop, search and question every fourth passenger leaving. Tommy and his fellow evaders were told that if one of them was apprehended, they should all break away from the queue, jump over the low wall that was about fifty yards away from the train and, if possible, escape to hide somewhere in the town. Fortunately, all of them got through safely. Tommy was lucky that the Frenchman immediately in front of him was checked. Once outside the station, one of Tommy's guides linked up with him again, and led him to a prearranged safe house. The party would only stay in St Jean de Luz for one day before setting off for the Spanish border. The brief respite was hardly long enough to complete all their preparations for the precarious long march that awaited them.

They were kitted out with berets and *espadrilles* (mountain shoes) and, as was intended, they looked very much like Basque peasants. Freddy and the girl (she may have been Dedee herself) had disappeared, to return to Paris presumably to continue their dangerous work. Albert remained, and he picked up a few more 'Basque peasants' as well as Tommy. They left St Jean de Luz on Tuesday afternoon in separate groups for the next safe place, a farmhouse at Urrugne in the foothills of the Pyrenees. It took them about two hours' walking. On the way, Albert and Tommy had to cross a railway bridge near Ciboure, and there they exchanged greetings with the German sentry guarding the crossing. From there they cut across country and reached Urrugne safely. They all met up at the farmhouse, had a meal, and then met their Basque smuggler-guide, Florentino. He was a tall, rugged man who only spoke the Basque language, a language, apparently, that is not related to any other. Florentino Goicoechea checked that everyone was properly kitted out and, in particular, that each traveller had a stout walking stick.

At nightfall, they set off in single file with Florentino leading and Albert checking that all was well at the rear of the small column. The weather could not have been kinder to them, for it was a moonless night. This suited their purpose admirably, and so they started their climb up the mountain paths. No one spoke. It was common knowledge that armed German patrols frequented the area searching for people just like them. At last, they reached the highest point on the French side of the range. Over the border, in the distance, they could see lights glittering. They could see very clearly, also, the lighthouse beam that swept the coastline near Fuenterrabia (Hondarribia). They sat together in a tight little group and took turns to swig from a bottle of brandy that Florentino had brought for them all to share. As they huddled together, Albert warned them that the next part of the journey would be especially chancy, and that they were not to move until Florentino had heard the sound of his 'lucky bird', which would be the signal that it was safe for them to venture down into the valley below.

The signal came, and down they scrambled until they reached a river. They approached it cautiously, and Florentino went up and down checking that the banks were clear. Some way up on the other side, they could see the Spanish frontier post with all its lights on. They knew that the Spanish police might be patrolling but they also knew exactly what they had to do. They knew, for example, that though they would have to wade in waist-deep, the River Bidasoa was fordable at this point in normal circumstances. After heavy rain, the swollen river became a torrent not at all safe to cross, as was proved the following year when one of the escape organisers was drowned. They held hands as they crossed. By moving as a chain, no one would be likely to lose his footing. There was no problem and they all climbed out. They waited a while to make sure that it was safe to continue. There did not seem to be anyone nearby, and all was quiet as they followed Florentino across a narrow road on to a railway track. As they were about to climb towards a welcome hiding place in some bushes farther up the bank, suddenly a voice screamed out for them to halt. This was soon followed by bursts of gunfire. They were being ambushed. They had been forewarned that if anything untoward happened, they were to retreat to the river bank. Tommy did as instructed, but got entangled in barbed wire in the darkness. He gashed the calf of his left leg quite deeply, but managed to loosen the wire so that he could carry on. Remarkably, this was the only injury of any consequence that Tommy suffered throughout the war.

When Tommy reached the river bank, Florentino was there already. They could only communicate by sign language, but they understood each other pretty well. No one else appeared. They waited five or ten minutes, then went forward cautiously to see if they could find anybody, but they were ambushed once more. They decided that it would serve no purpose to make another attempt, for the Spanish police would be fully alert by now. The two of them crossed the river back into France, walked upstream for a mile or so and crossed the border there. They climbed up steadily into the Spanish Pyrenees until they reached the summit. They did not tarry, but dropped down the other side as quickly as they could until they arrived at some gentler slopes and green fields. It was getting light now. They kept a sharp lookout for the Spanish police. They knew that they had stirred up a real hornet's nest. There was not much doubt that the frontier area was being scoured at that very time.

Since leaving the farmhouse at Urrugne, they had marched, climbed and scrambled for eight hours without much rest, so it was with great relief that they reached the next friendly farmhouse. It was still the dawning of the day, so they had to throw small stones against the upstairs windows to wake the farmer and his wife. Tommy and Florentino were welcomed with a hot drink and then led to a barn that they were to share with the cattle. They climbed up on to the floor above the cows, and stretched out in the warm hay that was stored there. They fell asleep at once. At mid-morning they were wakened and given bowlfuls of hot potato soup. They had second helpings as well, for they were ravenous. As soon as they had finished, the farmer returned to warn them to lie low as there were two policemen approaching the farmhouse. Florentino and Tommy peered through the window to see what was happening. Two armed policemen were chatting to the farmer and his wife, but they seemed very friendly indeed, and no wonder, for they had been greeted with a glass of wine each. However, no risks could be taken, so Florentino and Tommy left the window and covered themselves in the hay. About an hour later, the farmer came along to report that the visitors had departed in good spirits.

At midday, Florentino, by making various signs and pointing to his watch, let Tommy know that he was going to leave the farm, but that he would return in the early evening. Tommy dozed off in the hay. When he woke and looked round the loft, he saw a young family of rats playing. They did not worry him. In fact, they helped the long day to pass more quickly. At about 7 o'clock, Florentino returned with the news that it was time for them to bid farewell to their farmhouse friends. They walked downhill until they came to a main road, where there was a car waiting for them. Once settled inside it, Tommy relaxed for he knew that the next stop would be at the Consulate in San Sebastian.

Albert Johnson and the Polish airman were already there. Between them, they were able to give the Consul the names of the missing men who, most likely, had been captured. If that indeed was their fate, they would spend a week or more in a disgusting frontier prison while waiting for the Spanish authorities, first to admit that they had been imprisoned, and then to set in motion the usual slow release procedures. From the frontier prison, they would be transferred to a concentration camp at Miranda del Ebro, where they would be detained for a month or more before obtaining their release to travel to the British Embassy in Madrid.

However, Tommy was safe. After wallowing in a hot bath and savouring a deliciously cooked meal, he felt completely refreshed. The outlook seemed much brighter now. After breakfast the following morning, the military attaché from the Embassy met the evaders to explain the situation in detail. This was the diplomat who always collected the 'runaways' who had managed to escape the clutches of the Germans, and he would take them in his Diplomatic Corps limousine to the British Embassy in Madrid.

On the road to Madrid, at the entrance to every village or town, there were always armed police stationed to check travellers, but their official car was invariably waved through with a courteous salute. Once, they stopped at a road-house restaurant and thoroughly enjoyed a slap-up meal. When they reached the Embassy, they were lodged in a large army hut that had been erected in the courtyard. There, Tommy joined a dozen other servicemen, all waiting until clearance could be obtained for them to move south by train to La Linea, where they would cross over 'No Man's Land' to Gibraltar.

Meanwhile, it was very pleasant at the Embassy, even though they were confined to the gardens, and were unable to wander through the streets of Madrid. The attaché said that they would have to report to Police Headquarters to have their identities checked. They were given fictitious names and ranks, so that information did not get abroad that crashed airmen were finding their way into Spain from the occupied countries. Tommy was now Sergeant-Major Cook of the Army, and it was thus that he signed himself when he completed the form that would authorise him to travel through southern Spain to Gibraltar. On the following day, four of the evaders were escorted to the station where they boarded a train that would take them south. They were locked in a carriage with an armed guard on duty outside in the corridor. They were given coffee and sandwiches during the uneventful journey. What might have been a boring trip in normal circumstances was for them an exhilarating experience. At La Linea, they were marched to the frontier gates to have their documents inspected by the Spanish police for the last time. Tommy confirmed that he was indeed Sergeant-Major Cook. He was allowed through the barrier to cross 'No Man's Land' and then to step on to the British soil of Gibraltar. It was 21 September, the end of summer, and four weeks less a day since Tommy and Costello-Bowen had crashed near Antwerp, over a thousand miles away.

The four freed 'soldiers' were given routine medical examinations and billeted for the night. In the morning, their true identities were verified before they were given fresh uniforms and £5 spending money. At the Post Office they sent cables home. In her diary, Mrs Broom recorded the event on the 23 September. The next day she received confirmation from the Air Ministry that Tom really was safe. The entries in her diary, as usual, were understated, but it is not difficult to appreciate the tremendous joy with which she received the news that Tom had found his way to freedom.

At Gibraltar, Tommy had to wait for transport to take him back to the United Kingdom. Within a week of his arrival, he was reunited with a fit again Costello-Bowen who was very ready to celebrate the occasion with a beer. The first transport to become available was the battleship HMS *Malaya* and so, escorted by three destroyers and the occasional Sunderland flying-boat, Tommy and his comrades left the Mediterranean in some style on 3 October 1942, to anchor a few days later in the River Clyde off Greenock.

It was at about this time that 105 Squadron had been busy over Oslo. It was a while, of course, before Tommy heard about George Parry and Robbie Robson's escapade, of how they had disrupted a rally of Norwegian Quislings (collaborators and traitors) and bombed the *Gestapo* Headquarters, and of how the German fighters had left them alone at first, thinking that the Mosquitoes were part of the fly-past in honour of the parade! Neither did Tommy know yet, that notices had appeared in the local press about him at the beginning and at the end of September. They were precisely worded and gave no idea of the heartbreak and then the joyful relief felt by his family.

When they disembarked at Greenock, they were taken under guard to a local barracks from where they were escorted to catch the night train to Euston Station in London. Tommy was taken to the transit-camp based at the Grand Central Hotel in Marylebone, where he was interrogated by personnel from MI9 – the evasion and escape branch of Military Intelligence. He was then taken to the Air Ministry where, as well as being interviewed and given a written note of identity, Tommy was informed that 105 Squadron had moved to RAF Marham near King's Lynn, but that a Mosquito Training Unit was being formed to which he could be posted if he so wished. He liked the sound of it and readily agreed to accept the transfer to 1655 MTU. He was then issued with a travel warrant to RAF Uxbridge, where he obtained various documents and warrants before going on a three-week disembarkation leave.

There was an enthusiastic welcoming party for Tom when he

reached Old Posset. His brothers, Bob and Peter, were on special leave from the Services, and Muriel, his sister, had been given time off from the Bristol Aeroplane Company to join in the grand celebration. His old friends, Bernard Kristiansen, Tom and Norman Berg, and Jim Attwell, the landlord at the 'Old Vic', presented him with a congratulatory tankard that Tom still treasures. Of course, Tom's parents had never given up hope for his safety, and their delight so openly displayed was enough to make this by far the best leave that Tom had ever enjoyed. Mrs Broom showed Tom a letter that she had received from F/Sgt D.W. Evans, an old colleague of Tom's stationed at RAF Bicester, congratulating her on having such a marvellous son and rejoicing with her at Tom's escape.

Five years were to pass before Tom found out about the tragedy that befell one of the brave Belgian families that gave succour to the British airmen. In an emotional but restrained letter written on 8 June 1947 from the Chateau de et a Zellick, Brabant in Belgium, the Baron Paul Greindl wrote:

Dear Warrant Officer T.J. Broom,

My son, Baron Jean Greindl, was the Belgian chief of the line 'Dede' afterwards called 'Comete', which helped Allied airmen who fell in territory occupied by the enemy and repatriated them to England. His nom-de-guerre was 'Le Kas' then 'Nemo'. He was caught by the Germans, sentenced to death and imprisoned in the German Artillery barracks in Brussels, awaiting execution. Then in the Allied bombardment on September 7th 1943, he was killed.

I have found your name in the list of airmen whom the line was able to save.

You will understand, I am sure, how much my son's widow and the remaining members of the line would like to know what happened to you from the moment you had to abandon your aircraft until you reached England. We should all be most interested and very grateful if you would tell us anything you can remember of those days.

We hope that you have long since rejoined your family and we unite with them in gratitude for your safety and wish you all happiness and success.

In Tommy's logbook, there is but a brief, unemotional reference to the events of September 1942, but when he reads again and again the Baron's poignant letter, and reflects on what happened in Belgium a year after his escape, deep feelings of sadness and gratitude well within him.

As a matter of interest, in his logbook entry, no exact reference is made to the warship that carried Tommy home. Such information needed to be kept secret for, as there was always a danger that the logbook could fall into the wrong hands, the enemy might find out the whereabouts of one of the Royal Navy's battleships. It is worth noting, also, that the Officer Commanding's signature is that of W/Cdr Hughie Edwards, VC, possibly one of the best known names of the time.

Many, many years later, in a letter dated 6 June 1998, Tommy received an account of his crash from a Belgian researcher, Luc Cox. He named the area in which the Mosquito had crashed as the Paaltjesdreef, a lane bordered by oak trees behind which, at one time, there had been a pinewood. According to eyewitnesses, the fuselage and the two engines sliced a path through the pines. From his research, Luc understood that Tommy and Costello-Bowen had been helped by the nurses and the superintending doctor, Etienne Debaudt, of the Lizzie Marsily sanatorium for tubercular patients. He was fairly certain that the young woman who collected them was Dedee de Jong, and that they had had a drink in the 'Hotel Beukenhof', which still exists. To cap it all, Luc provided a map of the area!

In these days of continental holidaying, spending weeks in France or Spain has become an ordinary experience for thousands of British families. But during the war, Tom's escapades were made up of life and death incidents, and survival rather than enjoyment was the end in view.

CHAPTER NINE

Beer, Skittles and Mortality

As was mentioned earlier, 105 Squadron had moved to RAF Marham near King's Lynn by now. It shared the airfield with the newly formed 1655 Mosquito Training Unit, which Tommy joined in November 1942. The Unit had been formed to give specific training in low-level flying, before the crews were transferred to one of the two serving Mosquito squadrons, 105 or 139 (also based at Marham).

After some chopping and changing of personnel, by March 1943 Tommy had become the Chief Ground Instructor with Costello-Bowen as Chief Flying Instructor and F/Lt Robson as the Navigation Officer. They had been hand-picked by G/Capt Kyle and the dashing S/Ldr Roy Ralston who had taken command of the Unit. He had already won the DSO twice as well as the DFM. His partnership with Syd Clayton (also a DSO and DFM) was legendary, though by this time they had split up as Syd had gone on a pilot's course. With his inspiring leadership, the Unit developed into a most happy band of men who trusted each other absolutely.

It was in March 1943, also, that Tom received a letter from his brother Bob, now a Lance Corporal serving in the 2nd Lothians and Border Yeomanry with the Royal Armoured Corps in North Africa. In the letter, Bob gave advance warning that the next time they shared a leave together, he would 'duff' Tom up on the golf course. He promised as well that his next letter would be longer and more informative. Sadly, he was not able to keep his promises, and this proved to be the last letter that Tom would receive from his younger brother. A month later, Bob was killed in action and was buried where he fell at Mebjez-el-Bab, on the shore of Sugar Lake, and there he lies to this day 'resting where no shadows fall'. Mrs Broom received a standard, official notice from the RAC Record Office in Barnet, dated 11 May 1943, informing her that a report had been received from the War Office notifying the death of No. 7912347 Lance Corporal BROOM, Robert Henry, on 23 April 1943. The notice ended with an equally soulless expression of 'sympathy and regret of the Army Council at the soldier's death in his Country's service'.

In Mrs Broom's diary, dated 12 May there is a customary brief entry, but this time, the matter-of-fact brevity is heart-breaking:

'We had news from the War Office our dear Bob has been killed in action in North Africa. Muriel, Tom and Peter home.'

In a fine letter written by Bob's Squadron Commander, Major T.S. Robb, there was a kindly warmth that gave some solace to the grieving family. He explained that the regiment had been in action on that Easter Sunday, advancing to seize a ridge that had to be taken to allow the regiment to proceed. Bob had been the wireless-operator in the leading tank when it came under heavy shellfire just short of its objective. Major Robb ended his letter thus:

> *The loss of your son was a great shock to me. How much greater it must be for you. One can only hope and pray that this terrible war will soon end and that the world will never again be called upon to face such horrors.*

When Tommy returned to duty, he found that some important regrouping was taking place. RAF Marham was to become part of No. 2 Group, which had been set up to prepare for the invasion of the European mainland some time in 1944. From now on, the emphasis was going to be on offensive rather than defensive warfare as had been the case hitherto. The station and both 105 and 139 Squadrons were transferred, with their Mosquitoes, to No. 8 Pathfinder Group. Tommy's unit, as a result, seemed to be in a state of limbo. In May, 1655 MTU was moved to RAF Finmere as part of Training Command attached to No. 13 Operational Training Unit of RAF Bicester. The MTU had sole use of the new airfield, and it seemed to exist and to operate quite independently of other groups. Nevertheless, crews continued to be trained for operational duties with Mosquito squadrons.

At Marham, Tommy had been promoted to Pilot Officer. In the

past, it had been suggested to him that he should apply for a commission, but Tommy had been content with his rank of Warrant Officer and, especially, with his Presidency of the Sergeants' Mess – as happy a position in the RAF as a beer drinker could hope for! However, G/Capt Kyle pointed out to Tommy that, whereas commissioned officers were exempted from such duties as prisoners-of-war, if he had been captured during his escapade in France, he might have been forced to work for the enemy in some capacity or other. The thought horrified Tommy so much that he immediately accepted the advice, applied, and was given a permanent commission at once without any investigative interviews at all. This was a highly unusual preferment as only emergency commissions were normally granted in war-time. Not only that, but Tommy rapidly gained further promotion to the rank of Flight Lieutenant.

Tommy spent a most pleasant two months at Finmere, mainly because he felt so comfortable as a member of such an enthusiastic and efficient company of experienced airmen. At Finmere, he came across his namesake, Ivor Broom, once more. He had achieved the rank of Flight Lieutenant as well, and was now a Dual Instructor with the MTU. He wore a DFC ribbon, awarded to him for his outstanding service in Malta.

Further changes were being mooted, this time by Air Vice-Marshal Bennett, who needed a Mosquito Training Unit for his Pathfinder Force or PFF (formed in August 1942). He particularly required crews to be trained for the two Oboe squadrons and for the Light Night Striking Force (LNSF) squadrons. So it was that, in July 1943, 1655 MTU was posted back to RAF Marham, where Tommy had numerous old friends. He went ahead with an Advance Party consisting of a Sgt/Fitter, a Corporal and an Orderly Room Clerk to prepare for the move. 'Digger' Kyle told him that if there were any problems he should bypass the usual procedures and report to him directly. In fact, everything went smoothly and, within a few days, aircraft took off from Finmere to carry out their normal training flights, but landed at Marham when their allotted tasks were done. In this way, no time was lost in moving to a fresh posting.

In wartime, people had to learn rapidly, not only that life was precious, but that it could be forfeited at any time without warning.

On his return to Marham, Tommy was to suffer the loss of his long-time pilot and comrade, S/Ldr Costello-Bowen, in very unusual circumstances. A visiting officer at Marham, G/Capt Pickard, gaining experience on Mosquitoes after flying Lockheed Venturas, was asked by F/O Abbott of the Royal Australian Air Force if he could take the Ventura for a spin. He explained that he had been a Ventura pilot once and that he would love to have another trip in one. He invited Costello-Bowen to go with him to experience flying in such a fine aircraft. They took with them, for the ride, a Mosquito ground-crew man, Corporal Megson, as a special favour. Ten minutes later, Flying Control telephoned Tommy with the awful news that the Ventura had crashed. After all the frightening experiences that Costello-Bowen had been through, it was a bitter tragedy that he should have lost his life as a passive, though interested, passenger on nothing more hazardous than a pleasure trip. The three airmen were buried in the local graveyard with full military honours.

It was not uncommon during the war for servicemen to say of lost colleagues, 'Poor old so and so. He's got himself killed, you know,' as if it had been the deceased's own fault. After losing a dear brother and, now, a close friend, Tommy was not likely to utter such a comment ever again.

However, at the time, there was little opportunity to mourn absent friends properly but, before resuming normal routine duties, F/Lt Hoare did manage to thank Tommy for having refused him permission to go on the Ventura flight because of pressure of work.

Fifty years later, when he returned to Marham once more, Tommy stood at Costello-Bowen's simple memorial to pay his silent respect and, perhaps, to remember those hectic days when they had been young together.

S/Ldr Johnny Greenleafe came as a replacement for Costello-Bowen, and the Unit maintained its reputation for efficiency, so much so that Bomber Command sent an investigative team to find out how such a comparatively small team could be so well run. They left the station suitably impressed. Since the Oboe squadrons were operating from Marham as well, the airfield was for ever busy, day and night. Whenever they had time off from flying duties, they tended to heed the advice to 'eat, drink and be merry, for tomorrow we die' – a fatalistic attitude born of precarious existence and sad knowledge. With the exception of Ivor Broom, whose wife was lodging in Marham village, and who was, in any case, a confirmed teetotaller, they were all dedicated beer drinkers. W/Cdr Roy Ralston, a thoroughly enthusiastic leader in all things, led the way, but on the strict understanding that no matter how late the party ended, at roll-call in the morning, all crews were expected to report for duty fit and well. If the Commanding Officer happened to be the one missing at breakfast, invariably it would be Tommy and George Forbes who would go to rouse him. Roy Ralston had the reputation of being a great squadron commander. Those who served with him (never under him) would do anything for him. He was a much-decorated pilot whose good nature shone through to charm all who knew him. He had a ready wit and an interest in country pursuits, both of which were displayed when a senior officer advised him condescendingly not to shoot at a pheasant whilst walking. Back came the quick response, 'Of course not, sir, I'll wait for it to stop first!'

George Forbes was another popular member of the unit, for whenever he returned from leave, spent at Abersoch in the Lleyn Peninsula, he brought with him supplies of trout, salmon, lobster and game pie. The unit personnel lived like lords. As the Mess was rather crowded, the staff of 1655 MTU and some Headquarters people started using an ante-room to the dining room as their Mess. F/Lt Pascall was the Catering Officer. Before the war, he had been at the 'Trocadero' in London, and still had some useful contacts there. At about this time, also, one of the student Mosquito fliers was the son of a Sheffield butcher. If he was entitled to leave, or if he hankered for a long weekend at home, a lift could always be found for him. Airspeed Oxfords were used to practise the navigation techniques required by those aircrew who hoped to join the Pathfinder Force. An aircraft could easily and legitimately be routed so that it would land at a convenient airfield for one or other of the airmen. For example, Tommy's home was within easy reach of Whitchurch airfield just outside Bristol. By air, it took him 1½ hours to reach his destination, but if he had to travel by train from King's Lynn to King's Cross Station, then across London to Paddington Station to catch the Bristol train, by the time he got home, the first day of his leave would be over. To finance these convenient flights (and to provide a kitty to provide parties for ground crews), passengers were charged 1d (one old penny) per mile. There is no doubt that some of these flights enabled the privileged few to dine in somewhat superior style.

If there was a fog so dense that all aircraft were grounded, a party might go to King's Lynn, which was only about 15 miles distant. George Forbes had an old but trusty Opel that would take them, first to the 'Duke's Head' for a peaceful pint, and then to Mrs T. at the 'Nelson'. They made the most of these beery breaks, but then they worked hard and they did need to get rid of the inhibitions under which they operated at all other times.

Occasionally, when the fog was thick enough to restrict flying, but thin enough to allow them to run about, they would organise football matches. Of course, as a true leader, Roy Ralston selected and captained the team. In 105 Squadron, there was a Scottish International, Ian Macpherson, who was invited to play. After a couple of games, he was dropped. When questioned and criticised about his selection policy, Roy explained, 'Well, when Mac plays, he doesn't bother to pass the ball to me at all, and as your centre-forward, I'm the one who's supposed to score the goals.' Such was his popularity that the team accepted his reasoning as valid! A man who was to become nationally famous in later years was a pilot with 105 Squadron. Kenneth Wolstenholme was the BBC commentator at the 1966 World Cup Final between England and West Germany who shouted excitedly, 'They think it's all over,' and as Hurst scored again, 'It is now.' (Both Ken and Mac won the DFC.) George Forbes was a more than useful player who had represented the RAF pre-war as a full-back. The various anti-aircraft batteries stationed in the area had quite a few ex-professionals in their midst, so that they could have turned out almost a First Division league side if they had so wished.

The Anglican padre was the Reverend Bradford. George Forbes (clearly an influential man) had met him on a train journey from London and had started a conversation with him to pass the time. The Reverend let slip that he had not been too happy at the various stations where he had served as a padre. He had just been to see the Chaplain-General for advice, and it had been suggested to him that he should have one more try – at RAF Marham. There, he found his niche. He fitted in perfectly and all ranks enjoyed his company. The church was often packed on Sundays, and Tommy, with his friends, sat at the front to lead the congregational singing. Of course, it is likely that the fine spirit shown, reflected more credit on the Unit than it did on the padre's influence.

Very soon, Reverend Bradford's Christian compassion was tested to the full when he had to perform a most unwelcome duty. Ivor Broom had been giving night-flying instruction to one of the students when, approaching the runway to land, an engine cut out. Ivor took over immediately and was about to touch down safely when the student, presumably in a panic, seized the control column and yanked it back. The nose of the plane shot up into the air and the Mosquito crashed down to earth. The young man was killed instantly, and Ivor suffered a broken back. While the Reverend Bradford had to write letters of sympathy and comfort to the bereaved in Canada, Ivor was taken to the hospital at Ely, where he was encased in plaster from his neck to his thigh. He was there for some weeks, but seldom without company. He returned to Marham completely plastered (as a teetotaller, the only time in his life), and riding a bicycle! Once he was mounted and given a little push, he was fine, but the exit from RAF Marham led to a steep hill, at the bottom of which was a T-junction. His friends (and the padre, one hopes) prayed for his safety with some success, for he invariably managed to negotiate the junction without mishap. Within a few months, Ivor was flying once more.

Christmas came and went and all the station fared well with plenty of food and liquor. Christmas Day itself was exhausting. After visiting the Sergeants' Mess in the morning to be entertained, the compliment was repaid in the Officers' Mess before lunch. Then at midday, officers and NCOs served the airmen with their Christmas dinner and drinks. The afternoon was spent recuperating before their own dinner in the evening. On reflection, Tommy still finds it strange that he cannot remember any aggressive air activity from Christmas Eve until the day after Boxing Day either by the British or the Germans – and just as well it seems. However, it was not a quiet Christmas for everyone, for the 'Battle of the Bulge' in the Ardennes had started during the previous week.

Their time at Marham was coming to an end. The station's grass landing strips needed to be replaced with more solid runways, so 105 Squadron was moved to RAF Bourne, 109 Squadron to Gransden Lodge, and 1655 MTU to RAF Warboys, which was just a dispersal site in March 1944. They found their new station less than comfortable. The Nissen huts in which they were housed tended to be bitterly cold during inclement weather, but distressingly hot when the sun shone. To make matters worse, the huts were about a mile from the airfield itself, and all the dining facilities were near the runway. All aircrew were issued with bicycles. If nothing else, they were kept fit.

As Station Commander they had G/Capt John Searby. He had made his name commanding 83 Squadron in an attack on the Rocket Test Centre at Peenemunde in August 1943. This was meant to be a precision rather than a blanket raid, to be made by 600 bombers attacking in a series of waves. The errors of the earlier waves had to be corrected so that the following waves of bombers would be more accurate. Over this massively defended plant, John Searby, as Master Bomber, stayed to direct the other aircraft on to the target. As a result of the raid, the production of 'buzz bombs' and 'doodle bugs' was much delayed. At RAF Warboys, whether he knew it or not, he was known as 'Honest John', a lovely tribute to any man. At breakfast, he would sit at a table in the middle of the dining room. George Forbes and Tommy, very likely feeling a little guilty at being late for the meal yet again, would try to creep in unnoticed, but unfailingly they were spotted, and a voice would boom out, 'Forbes and Broom, sit here.' Not that they were afraid of him – they simply held him in great awe.

Though Tommy had been told by G/Capt Kyle that he need not return to operational duties ever again, he was beginning to have itchy feet (if those words are at all appropriate to define wanting to fly). After a brief preliminary discussion, he was offered a place with one of the Oboe squadrons, but Tommy declined, for their range was limited to the Channel-fringing countries and the Ruhr. He wanted to confront the enemy further afield. He went to see Roy Ralston for advice. Tommy was expecting to be paired up with F/Lt Burley, a fellow officer who also wanted to return to active duty, and with whom Tommy had made over a dozen training flights. Roy had another idea. He knew that Ivor Broom was thinking quite seriously about returning to operational flying. Roy had tried to dissuade Ivor from going back as he had already completed forty-five operations on Blenheims, most of them at low level. He had served at Malta where aircrew losses had been as high as 80 per cent. At one time, Ivor (still an NCO) had commanded 105 Squadron when all its officers had been killed or wounded. He had been commissioned in the field, and had gained an award for bravery. Moreover, Roy knew that Ivor was a husband and a father, but despite Roy's sound reasoning, Ivor insisted on rejoining a front-line squadron. In that case, Roy intended that he should have the very best of navigators, and so, with the Station Commander's blessing, a new partnership was formed.

CHAPTER TEN

The Flying Brooms

Tommy (from Rhondda Villas) and Ivor (from the Rhondda Valley), both Brooms, seemed fated to be together. Of course, their partnership had to be approved by Pathfinder Force Headquarters. They were interviewed by W/Cdr Hamish Mahaddie, another legendary character (nicknamed the 'Horse Thief' because of his reputation for scouring and raiding Bomber Command for talented crewmen) who had control over the appointment of all pilots and navigators wishing to volunteer for service in the Pathfinder Force (see Chapter 11). His response was positive. Ivor and Tommy asked for an opportunity to perform some practice flights together before going into action. They explained that they had only flown together once, and that had been in an Oxford when Ivor had taken Tommy to Whitchurch for his leave. Hamish scorned the request and told them to do their training over Germany! Despite this instruction, the two did manage about 1½ hours of air-testing and blind-approach landing in a Mosquito.

Towards the end of May 1944, they were posted to RAF Oakington a few miles north-west of Cambridge. It was a modern station with three concrete runways, and formed part of No. 8 Group of Bomber Command. No. 571 Squadron was commanded by W/Cdr Mike Birkin, a very fine airman who held the DSO and DFC Ivor and Tommy were in 'B' Flight, led by S/Ldr Johnny Greenleafe DFC who had joined the Squadron at the beginning of May. They shared the station with 7 Squadron, which flew Lancaster heavy bombers.

Within four days of reaching Oakington, and as part of the Light Night Striking Force, they took off an hour before midnight on 26 May for Ludwigshaven. This was the first time that Tommy had flown at night over Germany since November 1940. Apart from the usual searchlights and flak, they encountered little opposition and they landed back at base at 03.20 hours. (Though in casual conversation, airmen might say '3 o'clock in the morning' instead of '03.00 hours', in official records the 24-hour clock was always used.) Also in May, Ivor and Tommy took part in operations over Hanover and Leverkusen. In each of these raids, their Mosquito XVI carried a 4000-pound bomb (a cookie), which was dropped from 25,000 feet, a decidedly high-level attack but, according to photographic evidence, one carried out with accuracy.

At dawn on 6 June 1944 (D-Day), the long awaited invasion of the European mainland took place, but the Brooms were busy elsewhere. During the month they made twelve separate sorties into Germany, attacking targets at Leverkusen, Osnabruck, Ludwigshaven, Berlin, Gelsenkirchen, Homburg and Metz (via Saarbrucken). It seemed that 'Bomber' Harris objected to using his Command to support directly the forces taking part in *Overlord*. He wanted to continue with his strategy of destroying the Ruhr towns and Hamburg, and seriously damaging other cities like Berlin, Munich and Nuremberg. He believed that this policy would be more likely to end the war quickly, not only by denying the German armies essential supplies of war material but, also, by demoralising the German people as a whole.

During the early part of June, aircrews had been instructed to avoid an area in southern England that was marked by searchlights 'boxing' it in. This was where the glider force had been assembled in preparation for the crossing to Normandy. Tommy and Ivor heard all about it on the morning after the attack on Osnabruck. They were reminded of the occasion in 1940 when Ivor had been reprimanded by his CO for flying over a prohibited area near RAF Northolt in a Tiger Moth. When Ivor explained that he did not know that the area was out of bounds, back came the curt response, 'Of course you didn't know, it's supposed to be secret.'

During June, the 'Flying Brooms' completed five sorties over Berlin, the most heavily defended city in the whole of Germany. Hitler regarded any attack on the capital as a personal insult. The first raid on 9 June (in which 571 Squadron provided a third of the force of thirty-six Mosquitoes) lasted over four hours, counting the flight there and back. Tommy was not quite sure what to expect, so it turned out to be quite an experience for him. There was a total blanket-cover cloud hiding the target from the attacking force, so they were not much bothered by searchlights. However, there was an intense barrage of anti-aircraft fire all along the flight-path to Berlin. There was, also, fighter cover well above the bursting flak, waiting for an opportunity to pounce should the Mosquitoes come within firing range above the cloud. Some of these German night-fighters were Heinkel 219s (*Ulm* or *Uhu*, that is, Owl), which used a nitrous-oxide fuel-injection system. They were very fast indeed, and had been developed specifically to counter the threat of the Mosquito bomber. Ivor and Tommy, though, escaped trouble and returned to Oakington safely. Fortunately, this Heinkel fighter was not produced in great numbers. Preference was given to other aircraft, such as the Junkers 88, mainly because another Heinkel, the He 117, had gained such a bad reputation that it was known as the 'Widow-Maker' or the 'Flaming Coffin'. As soon as one He 219 had crashed, it was assumed that it suffered similar problems. There was another factor that contributed to its comparative uselessness, which was that it needed a special brand of synthetic fuel, and the plants that produced it at Wanne-Eickel, Homburg, Duisburg and Kamen had been attacked regularly by the LNSF. This, to some extent, proved 'Bomber' Harris's theory about denying essential resources to the Germans.

Ivor and Tommy were back over Berlin again on the following night. Whilst there were thirty-three Mosquitoes attacking various targets in Germany, the heavy bombers were attacking vital areas in France. Inevitably, there were losses. F/Lt Joe Downey had already completed forty-seven operations in Hampdens and Stirlings, but this was his first in a Mosquito with 571 Squadron. He was the proud holder of the DFM. His navigator, P/O Wellington, was on his very first sortie. On their way back, they were shot down by a waiting German fighter as they crossed the Dutch coast. They were flying at 27,000 feet and, having cleared German territory, were thinking already of their arrival at Oakington. There was a short burst of cannon-fire; the starboard engine was hit and it caught fire. As the Mosquito went down in an uncontrollable dive, Joe called out, 'Bale out.' P/O Wellington went through the bottom hatch. Joe tried to follow suit but could not make it. He was killed, but his navigator survived to tell the tale after spending a year in captivity.

The lesson was that no one could afford to relax at any time when on active duty. Even when heading home after completing a task, there was constant danger.

The following week, Ivor and Tommy were busy over Germany on three successive nights, so Tommy was not able to maintain the 'one night over Germany, one night on the tiles' tradition by drinking at the 'Red Lion' in Trumpington, or the 'Blue Boar' in Cambridge, or by carousing in the Mess. Many of the Mosquito sorties were diversionary attacks to draw attention away from the major raids planned for the heavy bombers elsewhere. These 'spoof' raids were not always successful. For example, on 21 June as many as forty-five Halifaxes, Lancasters and Wellingtons were lost in an attack on the Ruhr oil refineries. Of course, the Ruhr was such a strongly fortified area that it was not unusual for missions there to be severely punished. Aircrew, in their customary laconic way, knew it as 'Happy Valley'. On 28 June, whilst as many as twenty-eight heavy bombers were lost in a raid on the marshalling yards at Metz and Blainville, thirty-three Mosquitoes were directed to attack Saarbrucken. However, the leading aircraft had failed to mark the target properly because of a technical failure, so the Mosquitoes were redirected by the Master Bomber to Metz to do some damage there. The last entry in Tommy's logbook for June 1944 reads – 'METZ 22000 ft 1 x 4000 lb VIA SAARBRUCKEN!!!' S/Ldr Dodwell, whose VHF set did not function, continued on his way to bomb Saarbrucken!

A normal Tour of Duty ended after thirty missions, but for the Light Night Striking Force the number was fifty. Statistically, aircrew could not expect to survive that long, so life on a fully operative squadron was very intense. To ease some of the stress, they were given home leave every six weeks or so. Though the fliers themselves remained cheerfully nonchalant, seemingly unaware of the strain placed on them, others could read in their faces what they were going through. In his mother's diary there is an entry for July 1944, written at the end of one of Tommy's leaves, 'Tom is looking much better now than when he arrived.' Knowing Mrs Broom's gift for understatement, Tommy must have shown signs of real distress when he arrived home for her to have made any comment at all.

Straight after his leave, Tommy's first operation in July was to

Hanover on a raid that he described as 'fairly straightforward'. On 16 July, a few hours before he went on another sortie to Homburg, he flew with S/Ldr Terry Dodwell who, a fortnight before, had been awarded a Bar to his DFC by King George VI during his visit to RAF Oakington. The purpose of the hour's flight was to test some new bombsight equipment. Then, on 18 July, the Flying Brooms (in their personal aircraft – MM118) went for the sixth time to Berlin. It was an exceptionally busy night for, apart from the twenty-two Mosquitoes raiding the capital, there were other squadrons over Cologne, and heavy bombers attacking the oil plants at Wessling and Scholven Buer. They received a very hot reception at Berlin. There were fighter flares and red and green cartridges exploding all over the city. On the outskirts of the capital, their Mosquito was caught in a searchlight beam and was held in it, going in and coming out, for what seemed the better part of half-an-hour. This was evidently a radar-controlled beam. As soon as an aircraft was 'coned' by one of these, other searchlights would automatically be directed towards it. At the same time, radar-controlled flak would be pumped into the cone. In the cabin of their Mosquito, Ivor and Tommy, if they had had the time to spare, could have read that day's *Daily Herald* quite comfortably, it was so bright. However, Ivor was throwing the plane about to escape the danger until, eventually, he was able to level out in time for Tommy to direct him to the target. Their cookie was dropped onto the Target Indicators from a height of 26,500 feet. Then they photographed the damage inflicted on the German capital.

Sadly, that same night, there occurred a chapter of accidents that illustrated perfectly, though tragically, the irony of that trite saying, 'Such is life.' S/Ldr Dodwell, with whom Tommy had flown just a couple of days earlier, and P/O George Cash were scheduled to go with 'A' Flight to Cologne. For whatever reason, they swapped places with F/Lt Margerison (a Canadian) and F/Lt Clark, both on their first tour of operations, and down to go with 'B' Flight to Berlin. At dispersal time, the engine spluttered so that it was unsafe to take off. A reserve Mosquito had to be warmed up, which meant that they left some time after the others. Over Arnhem in Holland, they were attacked by a fighter that fired a stream of tracer bullets at them. They felt a few thuds, but as far as they could judge no serious damage had been done. They took evasive action and got clear. As they approached Berlin, instead of taking the planned run-in via Stendal, to make up some of the lost time they flew directly to the target. Suddenly, they found themselves in a thick stream of flak with shells bursting all around them. A chunk of shell came into the cockpit and smashed the Gee set behind the navigator's seat. Evasive action again took them clear. Now they were nearly at their target.

In the distance, they could see other aircraft being coned by searchlights and in trouble. George Cash had just enough time to record this information before moving into the nose ready for the bombing run. As he did so, there was a huge thump that made the aircraft shudder and jolt, but he managed to keep his balance somehow. He saw that the port wing and engine were a mass of flames, and that S/Ldr Dodwell was leaving the plane through the top hatch. Flames were licking round the cockpit and the Mosquito was going into a spin. George's plan had been to drop through the bottom hatch, but as he bent down he was pressed into his seat by the 'G-force', and at the same time his parachute fell into the hatch. Luckily for him, it stayed there and he was able to retrieve it before struggling back into the cockpit, climbing out on to the starboard wing and rolling off into space! He pulled the rip-cord ring, but nothing happened, so he tore off the flaps and the parachute opened. George Cash landed some 30 miles west of Berlin and was made a prisoner-of-war. His pilot, Terry Dodwell, did not survive. George found out afterwards that it was a Heinkel 219 that had finished off their Mosquito. It had been a hectic fifty-fourth operation for him.

It had been a hectic night for everybody else as well, but there was to be little respite for the Flying Brooms. After one day off, they went to Hamburg with twenty-five other Mosquitoes. F/Lt Thompson and his Canadian navigator, F/Lt Calder, were on their first operation with 571 Squadron. They were shot down, the latter losing his life in the crash. Also lost on the same night were twenty Lancasters involved in four separate small-scale raids.

The next trip for Ivor and Tommy was to Kiel on 23 July. Over 600 heavy bombers took part. A flight of three Mosquitoes had to approach the target some five minutes ahead of the main force to 'window' the flight-path with strips of tinfoil, with the intention of putting the enemy radar out of commission to allow the bombers a trouble-free time over the target. The raid was acclaimed as a huge success, for much damage had been inflicted at the loss of only four aircraft. Though to lose anyone was deplorable, the figures were a vast improvement on previous sorties. After scattering the windows, the Flying Brooms went on to bomb the target, and they did so a full minute before the Target Indicators burst behind them to show them where the target was! Considerable damage was done to the U-boat construction sheds at Kiel. A further aid to the success had been a complex spoof raid across the North Sea by aircraft of 100 Group that had scattered more radar-jamming tinfoil in German skies.

On the very next night, they were over Berlin again and encountered the usual severe reception. Tommy and Ivor avoided trouble both from fighters patrolling the Zuider Zee area on the flight-path, and from the searchlights and flak over Berlin itself. Not everyone was as fortunate. A shell burst in front of the Mosquito flown by F/Lt Mitchell and F/O Simkiss. It shattered and pierced the Perspex of the bomb-aimer's panel, causing a small fragment to lodge in F/O Simkiss's eye. Once they were clear of the area, F/Lt Mitchell applied a temporary bandage to cover the wound that was bleeding freely. They returned to base, where F/O Simkiss insisted on attending the debriefing session before going to hospital to receive proper treatment. He returned to flying duties the following February.

In what was left of July, there were more raids on Berlin, Hamburg, Stuttgart and Frankfurt. During July, 571 Squadron had been involved in 223 sorties, of which 214 had reached their primary target, including seventy-three sorties against Berlin. For Ivor and Tommy, their last trip was really eventful. They went into cloud at 7000 feet and climbed steadily to 25,000 feet. About halfway across the North Sea, the weather seemed to improve and the sky got brighter, so they expected to see moonlight when they broke cloud. Instead, the sky darkened dramatically as they flew into the anvil at the top of a thunder cloud. The aircraft went into a diving turn to starboard and lost height very quickly. Ivor showed Tommy that he was holding the stick and rudder to port, but to no effect. It was decided to jettison the cookie to lighten the Mosquito. After dropping steeply to 8000 feet, Ivor regained control and made for home. They landed safely at Oakington to bring to an end a month of contrast. Whereas the first fortnight had been spent on leave, during the latter half they had been on nine operations in just over a fortnight, a long sequence of 'one night on, one night off' that was an intense spell of activity. 'Spell' may be an appropriate term to define that passage of time, for it seemed as if their "Crossed Broomsticks" had the effect of bewitching the enemy.

They decided, however, not to leave things to fickle Fate, and the two of them consulted once more the Air Ministry instructions concerning ditching procedures when abandoning a Mosquito. As the navigator, Tommy had to:

1. Put IFF switch to DISTRESS position
2. Put Oboe transmitter in where fitted
3. Fasten safety belt
4. Remove collar and tie
5. Remove inner door of floor hatch (in case aircraft turns over on its back)
6. Remove Very cartridges and pistol and place in pocket
7. Disconnect oxygen tube and detach parachute harness if too low to bale out
8. Jettison top hatch on pilot's order
9. Detonate IFF, GEE, etc.
10. Brace for impact
11. After ditching, DO NOT RELEASE safety belt until all forward motion has ceased
12. Release safety harness and disconnect intercom plug
13. Pull main dinghy release
14. Follow pilot through top hatch, taking his 'K' dinghy and parachute pack
15. When clear of hatch, inflate Mae West
16. Board dinghy carefully, first passing pack and dinghy to pilot
17. Cut cord to free dinghy from aircraft

The navigator had to take on board his navigation bag containing about 20 pounds of equipment. He sat on his parachute and was restricted somewhat by his life-jacket (Mae West). All this made using the emergency hatches very awkward and, of course, even more so if window packages were stored. The pilot had a similar routine to follow but with more duties and responsibilities listed. Yet Ivor and Tommy managed to complete the 'abandoning the aircraft drill' in 40 seconds!

August started off much more calmly as the first four operations were cancelled for one reason or another. On 5 August there was a raid on the oil refineries at Wanne-Eickel in the Ruhr, followed by a trip to Cologne. Tommy understandably regarded Cologne as an unlucky target. He remembered having to bale out of a Blenheim in 1940 on the way back, and crashing in a Mosquito on the way there in 1942. This time, thankfully, nothing went wrong, and they returned to Oakington unharmed.

Quite a few distinguished people visited RAF Oakington as it was near enough to London for Members of Parliament to venture there. Tom remembers that after one of their many raids over Germany, he and Ivor met Anthony Eden, who proved to be a popular guest for he stayed up until 3 a.m. buying beer in the Officers' Mess!

CHAPTER ELEVEN

Radar, TIs and the Pathfinder Force

After the experience gained towards the end of the First World War, it was feared that there would be little defence against a huge bomber-force attack. Even with highly efficient fighter protection, because of the proximity of a potential enemy on the other side of the Channel, it would be difficult to organise retaliation in time. However, scientists were led to consider whether it might be possible to provide some advance warning of an incoming raid, and when they found that wireless waves could be bounced off targets in the same way that sound waves produced echoes, they suspected that the solution lay in that direction.

Robert Watson-Watt led the research and he experimented at Orfordness in Suffolk where there is now a bird sanctuary. After gaining some significant success, five radio-location stations were built along the Thames estuary. They were able to detect the Graf Zeppelin when it flew across Britain in 1937. At the outbreak of the Second World War in September 1939, a series of twenty 'Chain Home' stations had been built to cover the coastline facing the continent both in the east and in the south, stretching from Portsmouth to the Firth of Forth. Now, signals of approaching aircraft could be recorded from as far as 50 miles away, so that when enemy planes took off from airfields across the Channel, fighter squadrons were alerted and the pilots given crucial information about the attacking group's bearing, height and number. As we learned after the event, it was because of this facility that the smaller RAF just about coped with the *Luftwaffe* in the Battle of Britain.

'Radar' is an echo-producing system that works on the same principle as the one that allows a bat to 'see' in the dark by sending out signals that bounce back from objects in its flight-path, enabling it to avoid them. RADAR is an acronym for 'Radio Detection And Ranging', and it is quite appropriate for it to be a palindrome for the system involves sending a message and getting one back. High-frequency radio waves are transmitted and, when they hit an object, are reflected. This information provides the target's direction. The distance of the target is determined by how long it takes the short-pulse radio waves (travelling at the speed of light) to return. The information gained is displayed on the screen of a cathode-ray tube, and this happens no matter what the weather conditions are or whether it is day or night.

In the early summer of 1942, Tommy had been involved in testing Gee when he was at Gransden Lodge, and had become quite an accomplished operator of the system. Gee was a radar system that used a 'Master' and two 'Slave' stations that sent streams of pulses towards the continent. These were picked up by the aircraft flying towards Germany, and from the information obtained the navigator could track his course on a chart. It was claimed that by using Gee, the aircraft could be directed to within a mile or so of the target. However, since it took the navigator some time to interpret the signals received, the aircraft could have flown another few miles by then and accuracy could be lost. Also, the further away the aircraft went, the weaker the signals became and it was easier for the Germans to interfere with them. It seems that when Gee was used as early as March 1942 in a raid on Essen, the nearby towns of Hamborn and Duisburg were badly damaged! However, especially when used by gifted operators, Gee was a massive improvement on dead reckoning, the 'by guess and by God' method. In the 1000-bomber raid on Cologne at the end of May 1942, the first wave of aircraft consisted of Gee-equipped Stirlings that marked the city with flares. They were followed by waves of other heavy bombers in such numbers that a plane flew over Cologne every six seconds. Crews reported that the traffic was worse than during the rush hour in Piccadilly Circus. Despite this concentration of aircraft, there was only one mid-air collision over the city, which was lit up by huge conflagrations as 1500 tons of bombs were dropped in just ninety minutes. Some bomber crews claimed that Gee had little effect on bombing accuracy but, despite its limitations, it proved very useful to aircraft returning to their home base.

During 1941 and 1942, German radar was being rapidly developed. The Kammhuber Line was an early-warning radar grid covering the North Sea approaches and the Channel coastline. Each box in the grid had radar-controlled searchlights and flak, and was patrolled by its own night-fighter, which waited for a bomber to enter its sector like a spider awaiting a fly. The 'spiders' took a heavy toll of British bombers when first used. On 7 November 1941, for example, the RAF lost thirty-seven aircraft – 10 per cent of the raiding force. Though the Air Ministry denied the existence of German radar well into 1941, it seems that even during the Spanish Civil War, the need for some kind of radio navigation had been recognised, so that before September 1939, the Germans had experimented with radar. It is reported that when the British attacked Wilhelmshaven in the first raid of the war, the bombers had been spotted by radar as they crossed the North Sea.

The Oboe radar system (it hummed like an oboe) consisted of two transmitting stations set about 100 miles apart. The 'cat' sent signals indicating the proper flight-path by transmitting dots or dashes to correct any deviation right or left of the true path. The other station, the 'mouse', sent a signal to the aircraft when it was above its dropping point to hit the target.

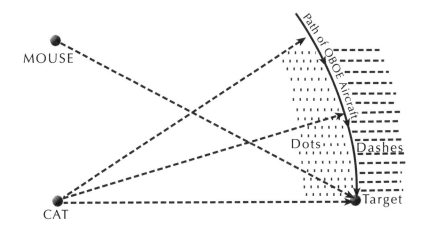

Oboe's main disadvantage was that the aircraft 'on beam' had to fly above 28,000 feet to enable it to reach its target about 300 miles distant. This was because of the earth's curvature. If an aircraft flew lower then it was limited to attacking a much closer target. Only one aircraft taking part in the raid carried the Oboe equipment and this plane would mark the target for the following bomber fleet. It was claimed that Oboe could guide aircraft to within a hundred yards of the target and, indeed, the Germans were much concerned about this sudden improvement, and suspected that enemy agents were signalling the aircraft from nearby villages. Oboe was first used by Mosquitoes of 109 Squadron in an attack on Lutterade in December 1942.

The Germans possessed a similar system, the *Knickebein*, which had been used in the early 1940s to destroy numerous towns in Britain. Of course, the *Luftwaffe*'s bombing was more accurate anyway because hardly any British towns were more than 50 miles from the coast. Navigation was fairly straightforward, as there were plenty of landmarks on the short flights from French airfields. British bombers, on the other hand, had to fly hundreds of miles to reach most German cities, which, apart from the northern ports, were far away from a recognisable coastline.

H2S was a radar system operated within the aeroplane itself. Pulse-beams scanned the ground beneath the aircraft, and the reflected responses were displayed on a screen to produce a kind of echo-map. As the system did not depend on receiving information about distance or altitude from ground stations in Britain, it could be used on heavy bombers as well as on lighter, faster aircraft. When it was first used, Lord Cherwell (scientific adviser to the Prime Minister) when asked for his opinion said, 'It stinks'. Very likely, Bernard Lovell, closely associated with its development and good-humouredly aware that the foulest smelling of all gases, hydrogen sulphide, has the formula H2S, may have re-christened it, for its original name had been 'Home Sweet Home'. H2S could distinguish water, coastline and town. In one sense, it could not be jammed, but it did have a critical weakness. When used over large cities, it received too many signals, so that it required a high degree of operator skill to interpret the information. H2S was much more effective when used to locate isolated targets or targets situated on the coast. H2S was first used in January 1943 in a heavy raid on Hamburg, Europe's most important port and Germany's second city. Subsequently, Hamburg was destroyed by further H2S-led bombing campaigns during 1943. During one raid, though, an H2S aircraft was shot down and its equipment examined in detail by German scientists. They developed *Naxos*, which enabled their night-fighters to home in on the bombers' radar transmissions. By the autumn of 1944, the British found it necessary to restrict the use of H2S because by then the Germans could monitor bombers' progress across the North Sea, long before they reached German air space.

Halifaxes of 35 Squadron based at RAF Gravely were the first aircraft to be fitted with H2S. Two Portishead men, Ray Davis and Jim Spedding, flew from Gravely with the squadron. They both regard 21 February with some distrust, for on that day in 1944 Ray was shot down over Stuttgart and spent the rest of the war as a prisoner, and in 1945 Jim suffered the same fate after a raid on Duisburg. There was one Mosquito squadron only that used H2S. It was 139 Squadron, which marked for the LNSF over Berlin (quite familiar to Tommy, of course). This squadron was at one time on active duty on twenty-three successive nights, certainly a service way beyond the call of duty.

A guidance system at which Ivor was acknowledged to be a supreme expert was known as the Standard Beam Approach. It was used to help aircraft returning to base in bad weather or at night. A beacon was set at the end of the runway to transmit Morse-code signals along the runway and beyond. There were two transmissions used simultaneously, one sending 'A' (.–) and the other sending 'N' (–.). Midway along the runway, the signals overlapped to give a continuous note. If the aircraft deviated from the correct course, the pilot would hear either 'A' or 'N' and he would then redirect his plane back on course.

The two systems Oboe and H2S enabled a bomber force to reach its target area with some certainty, but it was the use of Target Indicators (TI) that almost guaranteed a successful outcome. In the destructive bombing of Hamburg in the summer of 1943, yellow route markers guided the aircraft from as far as 80 miles out, whilst green markers were dropped nearer the target area, and then red followed by more green markers lit up the exact targets, which were the Blohm and Voss ship-building yards and the industries situated nearby. 'Candles' of high-powered flares on parachutes illuminated the countryside below. In this way, the guiding aircraft showed the flight-path to the hundreds of heavy bombers that dropped their high-explosive and incendiary bombs to create a firestorm down below. Gomorrah (named after the city destroyed by flames in the Old Testament) was the appropriate code word for this devastating raid. Yet, the citizens of Hamburg described the multi-coloured flares as 'Christmas lights'!

There were, basically, three kinds of Target Indicator. The 'Newhaven' was used when the ground was clearly visible. It consisted of a 250-pound canister filled with pyrotechnic candles of various colours. The 'Paramatta' was used to mark the target when conditions were unfavourable and radar had to be used. That is, it was a blind marking of the ground using Oboe and H2S. The 'Wanganui' was a sky-marker that was used when the target was completely obscured by thick, dense cloud formations. This TI indicated the release point that had been calculated, also using Oboe and H2S. For example, if the cloud cover was at 20,000 feet, the Pathfinders, using radar and allowing for aircraft speed and direction together with wind speed and direction, would drop sky-markers at 22,000 feet. The main force would aim for these flares knowing that their bombs would be likely to hit the hidden target. Of course, the higher up the marking, the less accurate the bombing was likely to be.

The LNSF Mosquitoes often bombed and windowed ahead of the main bomber force. A window consisted of strips of tinfoil (aluminium strips glued on paper) that were scattered in German air-space to upset the enemy's defensive radar systems. The window bundles were lodged between the navigator's legs. He was expected to dispose of them through a chute on the floor (in a two-minute period) before he could lower himself into the aircraft nose to use the bombsight, and to get himself ready for the run-in towards the target. German searchlights and anti-aircraft artillery were controlled by their radar stations, so that if the windowing was successful, the heavy bombers could complete their mission comparatively unhindered by accurate flak. The Americans and Germans called their window systems chaff and *düppel* respectively.

The 1409 (Met) Flight would report to Bomber Command, and the station Met Officer would then brief the crews about expected weather conditions and likely cloud cover over the target. Pilots and navigators would be told beforehand which TIs would be used. They could be of any colour or combination of colours and they would be changed every night so that the Germans would not learn to recognise regular patterns. Foreknowledge would have enabled them to set off mock flares to mislead the bombers away from the intended target. Tommy had the reputation for being the master bomb-aimer. He had attacked a marked target so accurately with a 4000-pound cookie that he had bombed out the flare itself – and he still has the photograph to prove it!

All these systems and facilities were regularly used by the Pathfinder Force of Bomber Command. When such a force was first mooted, the proposal was opposed by 'Bomber' Harris, who had no desire to see his squadrons depleted by having their star pilots and navigators withdrawn to form an elite group. Fortunately, his objections were overruled by the Air Ministry, and the new group was formed on 15 August 1942, under the leadership of Air Commodore D.C.T. Bennett. Just three months before as a Wing Commander, he had returned to Britain via Sweden after being shot down in an attack on the battleship *Tirpitz* anchored in Trondheim fjord in Norway. Don Bennett, very soon to become the youngest Air Vice-Marshal in the RAF at thirty-two years of age, was an Australian of vast flying experience. In October 1938 he had broken the world's long-distance seaplane record with a forty-two-hour non-stop flight from Dundee in Scotland to the Orange river in South Africa. Earlier in the year, and using the same Mercury-Maia composite aircraft, he had taken the first commercial load to be flown across the North Atlantic. The load was stored in the floats of the Mercury sea-plane, which had been made airborne on the back of the Maia flying-boat. Don Bennett landed the Mercury on the River St Lawrence at Montreal in Canada. When Tommy was serving in the Sudan, Don Bennett had been flying Imperial Airways flying-boats between Britain and Egypt. In the early months of the war, when he was still a civilian, he had ferried planes (Lockheed Hudsons) across the Atlantic, in winter, for service with the RAF. As a leader of pilots and navigators, therefore, he could claim to have done it all before, and that he knew very well what he was talking about. Though he was a forceful, opinionated man in some ways, and possibly unpopular with his more conventional superiors in rank, most of whom he had superseded, the men who worked under him knew him as 'The Great Don'. To them he was a living legend, almost a demigod.

There were very good reasons why it was necessary to form a Pathfinder Force of specially trained aircrew to be more effective in finding and hitting the right target, and only the right target. First, there had been much senseless loss of life among bomber crews in 1940 and 1941. Losses suffered in daylight raids had been so horrific that, by now, all Bomber Command raids into Germany were made at night only. Second, the vast majority of night raids were quite ineffective. Back in 1940, an observer is reported to have said, 'They used to tell us to bomb Krupp factories, but we got lost as soon as we left the airfield.' In 1941, only a quarter of the aircraft got within five miles of the intended target and a third of the bomber force got nowhere near it. So many of the bombs fell in cornfields that the Germans used to joke about how the British were trying to starve them into defeat. According to Group Captain Mahaddie, the bombing was so inaccurate that the Germans could not understand why some important potential targets were never hit. Of course, they did not realise that British bombers seldom located a target properly. In fact, after reading an analysis of bombing failure in November 1941, Churchill ordered the cessation of raids for a three-month period. It was evident that radical solutions were needed, and Don Bennett was the one to find them. By 1943, thanks to the availability of navigational aids and markers, a vastly improved bombsight (the Mark XVI) and, of course, the courage and persistence of volunteer crews, two-thirds of the aircraft would get to the target's immediate vicinity.

As an example of how it worked, on the night of 5 March 1943, a force of over 400 bombers attacked Essen where Krupp's factories were located. 'Bomber' Harris had ordered a prolonged onslaught on the Ruhr, and this was to be the opening sortie. Eight Oboe Mosquitoes from 109 Squadron led the way and dropped TIs on the target. They were followed by as many as twenty-two Pathfinder aircraft dropping further TIs at regular intervals to mark the target quite clearly for the three waves of Halifaxes, Wellingtons, Stirlings and Lancasters. In just half-an-hour, the operation was over.

Don Bennett only wanted men of skill, experience and courage to crew the aircraft that would spearhead the bomber fleets over Germany. When first formed, the Pathfinder Force consisted of five squadrons of heavy bombers but, because it proved to be such an effective force, eventually it comprised eight Lancaster squadrons (with H2S), two Mosquito squadrons (with Oboe), eight Mosquito squadrons of the Light Night Striking Force (139 Squadron having H2S in case the target was beyond Oboe range), and the 1409 (Met) Flight of Mosquitoes – the Weathermen. Though the original Headquarters was housed in some Nissen huts at RAF Wyton, where the first Pathfinder Force squadrons were based, it finished up at Castle Hill House in Huntingdon, a central position in relation to all nine airfields used by the Pathfinder Force.

There is not much doubt that the Mosquito was Bennett's favourite aircraft. He knew that a special relationship could be built up between the pilot and his navigator. They sat side by side, shoulder to shoulder, for most of every four or five-hour trip they did together. They could see what the other was doing, and every move they made seemed to bring them closer together. For this reason, Bennett insisted that Mosquito crews picked their own partners. There were other considerations to explain his preference for the Mosquito. It was highly manoeuvrable and, compared with other bombers, blisteringly fast. Its two 1680-hp Rolls-Royce Merlin engines could push the Mosquito to 415 mph at 25,000 feet. To avoid trouble, in an emergency it could climb as high as 37,000 feet. Yet, the 'Wooden Wonder' (designed by R.E. Bishop) could carry a 4000-pound bomb (the cookie), which was about half as much as a Flying Fortress, with its crew of twelve, could carry.

Later Mosquitoes were equipped with a device called Boozer, quite unsuitable for Tommy's fellow Broom, Ivor, who was strictly teetotal! A red light would show in the cockpit to warn the pilot that his aircraft was being monitored by German radar, but it was not all that popular with pilots because it tended to be on all the time when over strongly defended territory. Another radar device, Monica, warned if the plane was being tailed, but since it could not distinguish between friend and foe it was of limited significance, especially when an aircraft was flying in a bomber stream.

The LNSF Mosquitoes also went on spoof raids, that is, they

travelled with the main force towards the real target for that night, but some way from it they veered away to attack another with bombs and TIs, hoping to persuade the Germans to send up their night-fighters to tackle the Mosquitoes, and leave the way clear for the slower Halifaxes and Lancasters. The Mosquitoes could avoid trouble normally, for they were quite a bit faster than the Messerschmitt Me 110 and the Junkers Ju 88, but Mosquito crews could not afford to be careless for they had no way of defending themselves if they allowed a German fighter to get within firing range. The speed of the Mosquito allowed it to be used occasionally for daringly spectacular raids and, of course, these would be, deservedly, hugely publicised to raise the public morale.

Altogether, from the time it was formed until the end of the war, the Pathfinder Force carried out more than 50,000 individual sorties to attack nearly 3500 targets scattered all over Germany, but its brilliant work was carried out at the cruel cost of 3618 lives lost. The Pathfinder Force's work was fully appreciated by those in the know, and four of its stations (Graveley, Oakington, Warboys and Wyton) were honoured with visits by the King and Queen.

CHAPTER TWELVE

Swing Low Sweet Chariot

Hitherto, most of the raids carried out by the Flying Brooms had been at night and at high-level, usually well above 20,000 feet. Both Ivor and Tommy had had experience earlier in the war of low-level flying in Blenheims and Mosquitoes over the Low Countries and Germany but, though they had been on night-flying tests together, they had not taken part as a crew in low-level mining operations against the enemy.

Low-level training for special operations was carried out over the Fens in East Anglia, within easy reach of the Pathfinder Force airfields around Huntingdon. The aircraft would be taken up to about 25,000 feet, then the navigator would guide the pilot onto an approach path towards the target. When 12 miles away from the dykes, the Mosquito's nose would be put into a dive at a speed of approximately 300 mph. At 10,000 feet, the flaps would be lowered and the bomb-doors opened to slow the plane down to 230 mph or so. As they reached the Old and New Bedford channels, which stretched in a 20-mile straight line from Earith to Downham Market, the final approach would be made at a height of only 200 feet. Some pilots went lower. Bomber Command and the Air Ministry, understandably, received hundreds of complaints from the people living in the area, especially farmers worried about their stock, but there was little response apart from a polite letter blaming the 'exigencies of war'. As they were recognised as experienced low-level crewmen, despite not having crewed together before at low level, the Brooms were excused from the training schedule, even though it was in preparation for a special operation to be undertaken by Bomber Command.

The Dortmund-Ems Canal (168 miles long, 125 feet wide and 16 feet deep) was crucial to the German economy. Each heavy 500-ton barge could carry two train-loads of goods from the Ruhr to Emden on the North Sea coast or, linked up to the Mittelland Canal, could source the industrial areas of central and eastern Germany. It was estimated that, in the course of a year's trading, millions of tons of freight could be carried along these inland waterways.

As early as August 1940, an attempt was made to disrupt the traffic when five Handley Page Hampdens from RAF Scampton in Lincolnshire made individual low-level attacks with 1000-pound bombs on an aqueduct a few miles north of Münster. F/Lt Roderick Learoyd was the last man in and faced almost certain death, but he persisted against all the odds and survived the battering his aircraft received to be awarded Bomber Command's first Victoria Cross. Though the canal suffered a little damage, it was repaired within the week. Yet it was claimed that the raid had caused enough disruption to delay the invasion plans for some days.

Several other sorties were made in the intervening years. In September 1943, perhaps the most famous squadron in Bomber Command (617 – the Dambusters), flying from RAF Coningsby in Lincolnshire, attacked the canal with new 12,000-pound bombs (Tallboys). Near Ladbergen the fields sloped down to well below the level of the canal. A direct hit to breach the wall would flood the countryside and empty the canal. This was one of the most carefully planned raids of the war, but it was largely unsuccessful for traffic was only disrupted for a week afterwards. The canal wall remained intact but what was much worse, only three of the eight Lancasters returned to base – a tragically expensive operation, for as many as thirty-three men perished.

There was a particular reason why it was necessary to put the canal out of action in 1944. German submarines (U-boats) moored at Wilhelmshaven, Bremen and other North Sea ports had received a battering from RAF and USAAF bombers. In order to replace those U-boats as rapidly as possible, the Germans had built prefabrication factories in various inland towns where submarine parts were manufactured. Some of these prefabricated sections were so large that they could only be transported in huge barges along waterways. It was known that there was an important prefabrication plant in Dortmund, and that U-boat sections from there were taken on the Dortmund-Ems Canal to the northern ports for final assembly in vast, supposedly bomb-proof underground sheds with concrete roofs 7 metres thick. It would be disastrous for the German Navy if this important line of supply were destroyed, and the construction of replacement U-boats seriously hindered.

Now, in a combined operation with others, 571 Squadron was chosen to do the damage. On the night of 9 August, or more accurately, in the very early morning of the 10th (at 01.34 hours), Ivor and Tommy took off from Oakington. The plan was that they were to climb on track for Osnabruck at 25,000 feet. Just short of the town, Oboe aircraft of 105 and 109 Squadrons would release green skymarkers to the east of the canal to indicate a parting of the ways. Two Mosquitoes from 608 Squadron continued on the same flight-path to bomb Osnabruck, with the intention of deceiving the Germans into thinking that the town was to be that night's main target, as it had been many times before. Ivor and Tommy, with the rest of the force, turned and descended towards the canal. Red-spot flares, dropped by the Oboe aircraft some distance from the target, signalled that the height at that stage should be 1000 feet. From then on it was essential for the navigators to be precisely accurate. The mines were 10 feet long with a cylindrical diameter of 18 inches, and the 1500-pounders had to be dropped into a narrow waterway. Near Rheine, there was a 17-mile straight stretch of canal, so that from the red-spot markers 5 miles away, a timed run of about 90 seconds had to be made to bring them down to a height of 200 feet above the canal. Most crews actually flew lower to make sure that the mines really did drop into the water. To guarantee this kind of precision bombing, a cloudless, moonlit sky was needed, so that the water would reflect the shine. However, to their discomfort and danger, there was cloud at medium height and patchy cloud lower down. Navigators had been warned that there would be no room for error, so that once the clouds had been penetrated, decisions would have to be made rapidly. The Flying Brooms worked together like a dream, and the task was flawlessly accomplished. They flattened out, straightened up, and flew down a 3-mile length of the canal to the specified spot where they deposited the mine with inch-perfect accuracy.

According to Ivor, just before they released the mine, they had passed over a barge whose skipper almost froze with horror at these madmen skimming the canal. After the attack, they gained height rapidly to starboard. They saw one Mosquito receiving more than its fair share of flak. It was the one crewed by P/O Gent and F/Lt Dixon. Their starboard engine was hit, but they managed to recover height with just one engine operating, a tribute to the pilot and to the Mosquito's design team. The Flying Brooms made for the coast between Amsterdam and Rotterdam and, once over the North Sea, went via Southwold to base.

This had been Ivor's seventy-first operation against the enemy, a record of persistent courage for which he was awarded a Bar to his Distinguished Flying Cross. Tommy was on his fifty-first mission. This was his citation:

Recognition for which recommended – Immediate DFC

Particulars of meritorious service:

1. On the night of August 9/10 1944, Flight Lieutenant Broom was the navigator of an aircraft detailed to take part in the mining of the Dortmund-Ems canal. He navigated his machine with complete success to the markers and then made an accurate timed run to the point of release. Cloud and poor light added to the difficulties but his skill enabled the operation to be completed with speed and precision which completely surprised the defences.

2. Flight Lieutenant Broom has now completed 26 operations on second tour. He is a most reliable officer with a high sense of duty and responsibility and a member of a most successful crew. He assisted in the planning of this operation and his previous experience of low level bombing proved extremely useful. I strongly recommend him for the immediate award of the DFC.

12 August 1944

J.M. Birkin

Wing Commander Commanding 571 Squadron

The recommendation was immediately seconded by the Station Commander and confirmed by Don Bennett himself. In the fourth Supplement to the *London Gazette* of Friday 29 September 1944, there appeared the following Air Ministry notice:

The King has been graciously pleased to approve the following awards in recognition of gallantry displayed in flying operations against the enemy:

> *Bar to Distinguished Flying Cross*
> *Flight Lieutenant Ivor Gordon Broom DFC*
> *(112392) RAFVR 571 Squadron*

> *Distinguished Flying Cross*
> *Acting Flight Lieutenant Thomas John Broom*
> *(51227) RAF 571 Squadron*

In her diary Mrs Broom wrote, 'Tom has been awarded the DFC', as if it were an everyday event and, in any case, no more than her son deserved – which was true, of course. National and local newspapers were rather more excited and gave full and proper coverage to the story of skill and valour. Perhaps the most intriguing mention was made in a letter sent to the *Bristol Evening World*.

> *'Victorian's' note about floods at Portishead many years ago will be the more interesting now because a son of the boy who went to post in the washtub is serving in the RAF – Thomas John Broom – and has been awarded the DFC for gallantry. His many friends at Portishead will feel proud as well as*
>
> 'A SON OF POSSET'
Bristol 2.

It seems that in his younger days, Mr Broom had also made newspaper headlines – as a washtub sailor!

Ivor, expressing his appreciation of Tommy's skill, said that he was the most brilliant of navigators, and who better than a distinguished pilot to pay such a tribute to the man in whose judgement he placed absolute faith. With quiet humour he added that, even if they were not the first to take off, invariably they were the first to land, a comment on Tommy's efficiency and a wry hint that his navigator was ever anxious to be the first one back at the bar!

Of the ten mining Mosquitoes on the raid, two were unable to locate the target and brought their mines back with them. P/O Gent and F/Lt Dixon dropped their mine in another canal nearby, as it would have been too dangerous to return to the intended target with just one engine working.

Tommy's logbook entry was as concise as his mother's note in her diary had been, but with the addition of one seemingly incongruous word – 'gardening'. This referred to the 'planting' of 'cucumbers', a laconic way of describing a cheeky attack. The canal was closed for nearly two months, at that particular time a valuable contribution towards overcoming the U-boat menace. As a final expression of its importance, the Pathfinder chief, in his unashamedly partisan style, said that the mission proved that a Mosquito was worth seven Lancasters. In addition, he rather wished for the LNSF to be known as the FNSF, that is, to substitute 'Fast' for 'Light'.

On the very next night, they were back over Berlin, and that was followed by several more sorties during August. On 14 August they were over Berlin once more, and on the 16th whilst the heavy bombers were engaged at Stettin and Kiel, Ivor and Tommy were at Berlin yet again. The weather was appalling this time, with continuous cloud cover at 15,000 feet on the approach, some of it cumulonimbus (thunder clouds). As they reached the capital, they were met with such a ferocious stream of flak bursting around them that they could actually smell the cordite. Ivor threw the Mosquito about to evade this unwelcome attention, but they were hit repeatedly. They could hear the thumps as bits of flak hit them. However, they had to level out to make the bombing run and, after releasing the cookie, to obtain photographs of the scene below. This they did despite the continuing barrage, but almost immediately Ivor had to start weaving about once more. Tommy, of course, was in the nose of the aircraft being buffeted and violently thrown about. When Ivor called out for Tommy to give him a course to fly home, back came the cool, almost comic, response, 'Just fly West with a touch of North.' When Tommy had had time to work out a course, they left German territory and made a steady run home. Back at base, they inspected the aircraft and found that most of the damage had been to the wings. It was fortunate that by 1944 planes had been fitted with self-sealing fuel tanks, for their Mosquito had been holed more than once. However, their beloved Mosquito MM118, their trusty 'R for Robert' was no longer fit for service – after completing forty-one operations with 571 Squadron in approximately three months. It was repaired later, and was transferred in September to 692 Squadron.

On the next night, they were once more flying in German skies, this time over Mannheim – on a relatively trouble-free run. After a spot of leave, they were back in action in the dying days of August, attacking Berlin and Düsseldorf. On 5 September they raided Hanover, their last operation with 571 Squadron flying from RAF Oakington. During the summer months of June, July and August, they had flown more than thirty missions, including eleven sorties to drop cookies on Berlin. The other targets had been at Ludwigshaven, Hanover, Leverkusen, Osnabruck, Homburg, Gelsenkirchen, Metz, Hamburg, Kiel, Stuttgart, Frankfurt, Wanne-Eickel, Cologne, Mannheim, Düsseldorf and, of course, not forgetting their jaunt to the canal, a veritable geography lesson of a bombing tour. With typical service humour, the crewmen were wont to say, 'The RAF must never be accused of exaggerating. We have never worked more than seven days a week, and never for more than twenty-four hours in any one day!'

In his unusual publication about 571 Squadron, Barry Blunt wrote, 'Tommy and Ivor Broom were one of the Squadron's most distinguished and accomplished aircrew.' In the squadron that they were to join, they would fly again with 571, in joint operations, on at least a dozen occasions.

CHAPTER THIRTEEN

Night and Day

RAF Wyton, two miles or so from Huntingdon, was a pre-war station that had just been reopened with three new concrete runways. A new Mosquito squadron was formed with Wing Commander Burrough as its Commanding Officer. Ivor was posted to 128 Squadron as a Squadron Leader to be in charge of 'A' Flight, which meant that, to all intents and purposes, he was the second in seniority within the squadron. Sensibly, he arranged for Tommy to be transferred with him. As with their previous squadron, 128 Squadron belonged to the Light Night Striking Force of the Pathfinder Force.

The squadron was not to be officially on strength and ready for operational duties until 15 September, but since they had two Mosquitoes on station, they decided to go into action five days before they existed! Yet again, the target was to be Berlin. One Mosquito had engine trouble and its flight was aborted but, typically, Ivor and Tommy took off anyway. Berlin's defence units were extremely aggressive with intense anti-aircraft fire, numerous searchlights and many aircraft coned. Despite the dummy flares set off near Magdeburg, the raid was completed satisfactorily.

No. 128 Squadron was equipped with Canadian-built Mosquitoes (Type XX, which carried 4 x 500-pound bombs but, gradually, the squadron was being re-equipped with the more favoured Mosquito Mk XVI, which could carry a 4000-pound cookie. New crews were arriving as well, and Ivor, as Flight Commander, was kept busy acclimatising them to life in a fully operational Mosquito squadron, for most of the crews had come directly from 1655 MTU (the Flying Brooms' old unit). Ivor and Tommy could not now go on missions at the same hectic pace as before. They had other responsibilities, with Ivor overseeing the fresh young pilots and Tommy involved in advising the new navigators. However, the two of them did manage one uneventful trip to Brunswick before they went on leave.

In October, there were raids on Berlin, Hanover and Essen. This last engagement on 23 October was planned to be the heaviest bombing raid ever, with more than 1000 aircraft taking part. Ivor, by now, had taken over a Type XVI Mosquito (PF401), a sort of replacement for their beloved old 'R for Robert' with its 'Crossed Broomsticks' symbol. Very soon after take-off, they came across a layer of stratus cloud between 10,000 and 12,000 feet and, over the Ruhr, a thicker cloud-cover higher up as well. Ivor and Tommy windowed ahead of the main bomber stream, carried out their own bombing, then stayed around as previously instructed to assess the quality of the attack. It was fortunate that skymarkers had been dropped, as the other Target Indicators had burst well below cloud level and were not visible to the heavy bomber crews.

In addition, many skymarkers were scattered over an unusually wide area, causing Ivor and Tommy to conclude that the raid, despite its intended intensity, would not be entirely successful as it was not adequately concentrated. They set course for home on the most direct route to make their report. Air Vice-Marshal Bennett was waiting for them in the Operations Room. Immediately, he conveyed their views to Air Chief Marshal Harris who accepted their report without question and, subsequently, ordered another major attack on Essen to be carried out. If any proof were needed of the high esteem in which they were held, this was powerful evidence that the Flying Brooms were men whose word commanded respect.

At the end of October, Berlin was once more targeted. Tommy had observed that the last three operations had taken off comparatively early – at 18.17, 17.29 and 17.32 hours, that is, not long after tea-time. Ivor explained that he had calculated, since their missions usually lasted between 4 to 4½ hours, how they could claim to have been to Berlin and back before the bar closed and that, of course, he had thought all this out for Tommy's benefit! During the month, the two of them had been on but four operations, a dramatic slowing down of the pace of activity they had become accustomed to during the summer months.

On the first night of November, 128 Squadron raided Berlin. The

Mosquitoes flew to Cromer on the east coast, crossed the North Sea to the west of Heligoland, and flew down between Hamburg and Kiel to a point north-east of Berlin. From there they made a 20-mile run-in to the city. Down below, the squadron had been closely tracked by German radar and it was evident that the capital was to be the target. As the weather was fine and cloudless, night-fighters scoured the skies for them but, despite all the attention paid to them by plane, searchlight and flak, the nimble Mosquitoes enjoyed almost a trouble-free operation.

On Guy Fawkes' Night, Stuttgart was to suffer that year's firework display. The Mosquitoes took a route that was much safer. From Wyton, they made for Orfordness and then flew directly to the target over mainly friendly territory. By this time, most of France had been freed from German occupation and the Allied armies had reached the Rhine. However, they still had to be wary of fighter-planes. This comparatively comfortable flying only applied to trips over southern Germany. Attacks in the north of the country always entailed long periods over heavily defended areas, for the Germans still held Holland. The return flight from Stuttgart across Luxembourg and Beachy Head was a nice, gentle excursion according to Tommy's report.

There was another operation on 11 November (the 1914–18 Armistice Day) with about forty Mosquitoes targeting the oil refinery at Kamen in the Ruhr. At the same time, over 200 bombers attacked Dortmund and Harburg nearby. After a brief leave, Ivor and Tommy were back in action over Nuremberg on 28 November. As many as seventy-one Mosquitoes, including six Oboe aircraft, took part in this raid deep into southern Germany. The target had been accurately marked so that the bombing was really concentrated on the engineering factories, with a total bomb-load of about 200,000 pounds of explosives causing immense destruction. Perhaps even greater damage was inflicted on German morale, for Nuremberg was the city most favoured by the Nazis. It was here that they held their party rallies each year, with banners aloft, chanting crowds and an adoring populace 'heiling' Adolf Hitler, their Leader. Nuremberg symbolised the greatness of the Third Reich, but this raid signalled to the German people that what had been promised and guaranteed to last a thousand glorious years would end ignominiously very soon. It had all been an empty boast. So successful was this raid that all the squadrons that had taken part were sent congratulatory messages from 8 Group Headquarters.

With the end of November came a change of tactics. The LNSF, contrary to its style, was to be used for daylight bombing of industrial targets. The first mission was to Duisburg to destroy the Benzol production plant there. In another combined-squadron operation, the force totalled thirty-eight aircraft, with six Oboes. The Flying Brooms led 128 Squadron at the head of the force. Air Vice-Marshal Bennett had issued precise instructions regarding airspeeds, but Ivor disagreed and, as leader, decided to stick to their proven formula for successful sorties. They would take off, climb and get into formation quickly, then *rendezvous* with the Oboe aircraft at the agreed position, height and time somewhere over the North Sea. The Oboes would be on beam already, so that all the formation had to do was to follow, and bomb as indicated by the flares. As soon as they took off, Ivor asked Tommy to make a quick check that all aircraft were accounted for. Tommy reported that, as far as he could judge, all seemed to be in order except that, for some unaccountable reason, a Bristol Beaufighter was tailing them. Everything went according to Ivor's plan. They picked up the Oboe Mosquitoes, exchanged recognition Very flares, and proceeded on course. Not a minute was wasted. (A minute wasted could mean a 5-mile inaccuracy at the speeds they travelled.) They had fighter cover above them and, though there was a flak barrage, not a single Mosquito was lost. Cloud cover hid the target, but they bombed on the Target Indicators, turned away and set course for home. Tommy looked behind as they left Duisburg. Suddenly, a huge column of brownish-black smoke pierced the cloud at 10,000 feet, a sure sign that the Gessellschaft Teerverwertung Benzol plant had been badly damaged. The thirty-two Mosquitoes, each dropping a 4000-pound cookie on a small target in about half-a-minute, must have caused much havoc as well as massive damage.

The following day, national newspapers carried flattering reports of the raid, and praised in glowing terms the brave crews. However, at RAF Wyton when they got back, Ivor was on the carpet. Air Vice-Marshal Bennett was waiting for them and wanted to know exactly why his instructions regarding airspeeds had been ignored. He made it quite clear that, to say the least, he was very unhappy. After all, he had joined the mission to see his men in action, and it was not often that officers of his rank went into battle. Of course, it was he who had been in the extra Beaufighter spotted by Tommy but, because Ivor had not followed his flight plan, his aircraft had been unable to keep up with the much nimbler Mosquitoes. The 'Great Don', despite his keenness, had seen nothing of the brilliantly successful attack on Duisburg. It was no wonder that he was peeved. Fortunately, Ivor knew what he was about and explained precisely why he had disregarded the unsuitable orders that he had been given. This response to an angry Air Vice-Marshal required some courage, but then Ivor had never lacked that quality of character. The sequel was that the instructions for the following day's daylight raid quoted Ivor's preferred speeds.

The daylight attack on Duisburg, with its heavily defended, vital war-time industries, showed open contempt for the Germans' ability to counter such a raid, and it emphasised the significance of the previous raid on Nuremberg. It was the clearest sign yet to German civilians that the war would never be won by them, no matter how much their Leader ranted. The Duisburg raid, also, had been Ivor and Tommy's forty-fourth operation on this particular tour of duty (Ivor's eighty-ninth and Tommy's sixty-ninth in total), a tremendous feat of endurance and good fortune. Yet the two of them were fretting that when they reached their fiftieth together, they would be grounded! It so happened that they were allowed to extend their tour, to continue together as the Flying Brooms until the end of the war.

On the first night of December, with the LNSF once more, they raided Karlsruhe, a trip described by Tommy as 'nice and easy', presumably because it was over Dieppe and Allied-held territory again. On 11 December, in an Oboe-led attack, they made a daylight raid on Hamborn in the Ruhr. The Mosquito's versatility was certainly tested on this occasion, for they had a passenger on the flight, Major Mulloch, a Royal Artillery liaison officer at 8 Group Headquarters. Tommy stayed put in his seat alongside Ivor while the Major occupied the bomb-aimer's position in the nose of the Mosquito. There, he had a fine view of everything, including all the bursting flak aimed at them. The Major was given the extra privilege of releasing the cookie. They enjoyed the uneventful trip back to base, and they surely enjoyed the bacon and eggs they had at midday, as well as the little celebration they shared with the Major, who had been exhilarated by his experience. He was shocked to learn, though, that two of the crews would be back over Germany again that night. However, Ivor and Tommy had a short leave due to them, and they did not fly again until 23 December when the target was Limburg. Being on such a mission within a few hours of Christmas Day was not a joyous affair, but it did not dissuade them from enjoying a rousing festival two days later.

CHAPTER FOURTEEN

Tunnel Vision

As a final fling to secure victory from almost certain defeat, the Germans counter-attacked on the Ardennes front in the Belgian–French border region, which was as weakly held in 1944 as it had been in 1940. The Ardennes was a hilly, wooded area unlikely to be attacked by tank formations, so it was only defended by four, rather depleted, US Infantry Divisions. However, the Germans did the unexpected again and, on the night of 15 December, they *blitzkrieged* the region with twenty-eight divisions (including nine Panzer divisions) with six further divisions ready for a follow-up attack. The German aim in what became known as the 'Battle of the Bulge' was to cut through the Allied armies, in particular to split the US First and Third Armies, encircle them, drive to the coast to cut off General Montgomery's 21st Army Group, and then capture the port of Antwerp. They intended inflicting such damage that the Allies would have to think again about the wisdom of risking even greater losses if they ventured into Germany itself.

The initial thrusts were so effective that the Allied armies were driven back. Within ten days, the US armour and infantry had been chased 60 miles towards the River Meuse. The Germans began to think that their operation (code-named *Nacht Am Rhein*) might even convince the British and Americans to seek a truce. The main problem for the advancing Panzer tanks was how to get adequate supplies of fuel to maintain the momentum. The southern German rail system was crucial in this respect. As many as 800 specially commissioned trains carried supplies from the Koblenz and Cologne areas but, as Bomber Command was well aware, most railways, at one place or another, need tunnels to take them through obstructing hills. If the tunnels in the Eifel region of Germany and in the Ardennes hills could be put out of use, it would be a severe setback to German plans by disrupting their lines of essential supply. No. 128 Squadron was chosen to attack nine of the tunnels, and 692 and 571 Squadrons were detailed to target others. Operation *Boring* was scheduled for New Year's Day 1945.

Not unexpectedly, Tommy was celebrating Hogmanay in the Officers' Mess, so Ivor did not have to waste much time searching for him. He tapped Tommy on the shoulder and ordered him to bed to be ready for an early morning call at the dawning of the New Year. It is true that Tommy did retire earlier than usual, but not before he had sneaked another couple of 'auld lang syne' pints. Come 6.30 a.m. though, when they took off, he was prepared for whatever was to befall that day.

The Flying Brooms were to attack the tunnel at Kaiserslautern, the link between Mannheim and Saarbrucken, that supplied the eight German divisions employed in the Saar area. This would be a hazardous operation, for the best chance of getting a 4000-pound cookie into the tunnel was by skip-bombing, that is, flying down to ground level, tossing the bomb into the tunnel entrance, then climbing steeply away – and rapidly, for never before had a cookie been dropped at such a low level. To minimise the danger, delayed fuses were used, to allow the crew some ten seconds to escape the bomb blast. Tommy's navigation was as superb as ever and, with deadly accuracy, he led Ivor to the Kaiserslautern tunnel in the shortest possible time. Wisely, they attacked from the German end of the tunnel, so that if any mishap occurred, at least they would be flying towards friendlier territory. Ivor took the Mosquito down close to zero level, narrowly missing telegraph poles and railway signals. He released the cookie into the mouth of the tunnel just after a freight train had entered it. As soon as the heavy load was deposited, the Mosquito shot up a couple of hundred feet anyway but then, with consummate skill, Ivor banked the aircraft steeply, and over the hill they went. There was a massive explosion below. Rear-view photographs provided evidence of their brilliant escapade. Not one of the takes showed a train leaving the tunnel! Until they examined the photographs in greater detail later, they were unaware that they had been chased by two Fw 190s out for vengeance. So, as it was 08.30 hours on the first day of 1945, they broke radio silence to wish all crews in 128 Squadron a 'Very Happy New Year'. Of course, they did not know then that one crew had not survived to live another year. F/Lt Wellstead and F/Lt Mullen (in their Mosquito P411) had crashed on take-off.

Ivor gained a second Bar to his DFC. The Bar to Tommy's DFC was cited thus:

Flight Lieutenant Broom DFC was a navigator in a Mosquito aircraft of 128 Squadron detailed to place a 4000 lb bomb up to the mouth of a railway tunnel in the region of Kaiserslautern on the morning of the 1st of January 1945. This operation required great skill, determination and the utmost precision. By his assistance to his pilot this attack was carried out most successfully. Flight Lieutenant Broom has completed 73 operations against German targets, the majority of which were heavily defended and including 15 against Berlin. He has, at all times, shown consistent keenness and skill.

The Station Commander supported the recommendation by emphasising Tommy's fine spirit and complete disregard for enemy opposition. The reason for the award was kept secret, and the newspaper reports made no reference to the Kaiserslautern tunnel. Nor did the press indicate how out of the ordinary it was for a pilot to win three gallantry awards, and how even more unusual it was for a navigator to win two.

The German advance in the Ardennes was frustrated by the lack of adequate supplies, and the divisions were halted eventually when they failed to capture Bastogne, bravely defended by US divisions. On 12 January the operation was abandoned, and by the end of the month the Battle of the Bulge was over.

After some leave, Ivor and Tommy, in the company of 571 and other squadrons, went to Berlin again – their last operation with 128 Squadron. As usual, they left behind a cookie calling card. By the time they got back to RAF Wyton, the weather had deteriorated so badly that the conditions were quite nasty, with a thick cloud base of only 300 feet and visibility down to less than 800 yards. Less skilful pilots and navigators would have been instructed to abandon their aircraft rather than attempting to land in such atrocious weather. (If visibility had been affected by thick fog, they would have been diverted to Gravely or Downham Market where FIDO was operated. The Fog Investigation and Dispersal Operation consisted of fog-clearing burners scattered around the airfield and in particular along the edges of the runways, so that these stations were always available for emergency landings in such weather.) However, Tommy had become really expert at interpreting the pulses on his Gee radar set, and he had noted that one of the grid lines on the chart coincided with the runway at Wyton. In any case, Ivor had no qualms about making a safe landing, which he did, so that their return to RAF Wyton had only been a near-disaster! Other crews had not been so fortunate. The Mosquitoes involved in this Berlin raid suffered the most losses ever. Two crews baled out over the Wash, three crashed in Belgium and another five in England.

Tommy had been with 128 Squadron for four months, but in that brief period he had become one of its most popular members. In the first place, he was admired for his proven skill and courage in the face of the enemy. Then he was respected for his career in the RAF in which he had served since 1932 and risen through the ranks. There was hardly anyone else around who had enjoyed a more varied experience of service life than Tommy. He was some years older than most of his fellow airmen. At thirty, he seemed quite ancient to the youngsters, most of them in their late teens or early twenties, but he was young at heart and ever willing to stand his round(s) whenever there was cause for celebration.

His colleagues knew Tommy as the man described twelve years earlier as 'most trustworthy, intelligent and courageous' but they would not have recognised him as the 'sober young man' whom Dr Wigan had praised so highly. They knew him as the friend who would drink Ivor's beer for him, after he had drunk his own of course. Rumour has it that, for once in his life, Tommy had fallen asleep through exhaustion and alcohol, possibly. His lively companions made the most of their opportunity and shaved off Tommy's precious moustache while he slept soundly in his bed. The 'Weathermen' of Flight 1409 were particularly happy to join in the spirit of the occasion, and between them composed some verses entitled: 'A Brief Ode To A Lost Fungus'.

> He wore it proudly, much as men
> Will wear their leek and thistle.
> But Ichabod! there's nothing worse
> Than a Broom without a bristle.

He stands but half the man he was
Around the crowded bar –
Like some Clipper, beauteous once,
Now stripped of sail and spar.

His story rings a little strange –
That some low, dirty dog
Stalked him when he left the Mess,
And snatched it in the fog.

Again, we've heard that yesterday
It was quite cold, and froze.
It broke in twenty pieces, when
He tried to blow his nose!

Oh tell us, please, that by the Spring,
'Twill burst and bloom again,
In richer glory than the growth
Which met the dirty drain.

Grow it Tommy. In this Mess
Are many mad and queer.
You alone looked as we should
Behind a mug of beer.

As if the previous ode had been a hastily composed, inadequate tribute to Tommy's moustache, there followed a few more verses of hope for the future, as some wisps of hair started reappearing. The title was Miltonic, 'Paradise Regained', and the poem's dedication was:

To one Thomas Broom, Spiritual and Cultural leader of Squadron
No. 128 from the members of 1409 Flight.
It burst in bounteous raggedness,
From whence no man can tell.
Quite seasonless, a lovely growth

In winter's icy spell.

Tenderly, with precious care
Each little bristle grew.
Each showing from its very birth
The will to bloom anew.

But whence its strength? From what deep seat
Can this fine spirit spring?
Which, in short weeks, makes Armstrong's look
A trickle of a thing.

In just a month, he well could whack
All other sorties flown.
A goodly sprint – and he could make
A take-off on his own.

Trim it not; but this time, let
Its sweeping grandeur flow,
Its ends uplifted to the stars,
Its centre – toecap low.

Keep it strong and fine and free,
Beyond all human match.
Where birds may nest, and maidens come
To shelter 'neath its thatch.

But lest in endless beer and smoke
The lesser bristles bleach,
Just one last plea.....another pipe
Of slightly longer reach!

Though the unknown poet had an Auden-like understanding of rhythm and rhyme, the verses have greater significance than that, for they capture the spirit of the time, when honour was given to an 'ordinary' man in extraordinary circumstances. The Weathermen knew that the very next day, perhaps, Tommy might be killed in action, and that they themselves might not be alive to mourn him. Yet they took the trouble, and much pleasure, to pen these, on superficial reading, trivially humorous odes. Of course, with more thoughtful study, they show a depth of feeling, a true comradeship, which they would have been too embarrassed to express in a more direct fashion. Yet these were all brave men. 1409 (Met) Flight of Bomber Command flew unarmed Mosquitoes deep into German territory daily. One of the Flight's planes completed nearly two hundred missions and, of course, had the appropriate number of symbols painted on its fuselage. As the result of their outstanding work, RAF Wyton became known as the finest weather station in the whole of Britain!

It may not be inappropriate for the author to record here his experience in 2006 when he accompanied Tommy Broom and Lady Broom (the late Ivor Broom's wife) to RAF Wyton to attend the Pathfinder Memorial Service. It seemed quite clear that despite the passage of over sixty years, Tommy was remembered with affection, for a long-service Warrant Officer even knelt before him to be blessed! After the Memorial Service, the congregation gathered in a nearby field to witness a fly-past by an Avro Lancaster. It hardly needs saying that there were numerous misty-eyed spectators there with long, affectionate memories of distant days and lost comrades.

CHAPTER FIFTEEN

The Grand Finale

Quite soon after receiving a congratulatory telegram from Air Chief Marshal Harris, the time came for Ivor and Tommy to leave 128 Squadron. To describe the transfer as a move would be an exaggeration, for all they had to do was to take over a hangar at RAF Wyton. As an example of how forceful Don Bennett could be, Ivor was called in to see him at tea-time one afternoon and told, 'You will form 163 Squadron at Wyton tomorrow so that you will be ready for your first action tomorrow night.' At the time, of course, the newly formed 163 Squadron had no aircraft, no aircrew (apart from Ivor and Tommy, that is), and no ground crews or office staff. Overnight, though, personnel were drafted, and the Squadron was established with two Mosquitoes. Ivor intended operating immediately, but poor weather intervened and the Squadron's first action was delayed for a day. From 25 January 1945 then, Ivor was promoted to be Wing Commander in charge of the new squadron, and Tommy was made Squadron Leader to be responsible for all the navigators. They were joined by 'Dizzy' Davies, a former solicitor, who became the Squadron's adjutant with responsibility for non-flying matters. Ivor never failed to emphasise that the Unit's success depended just as much on Dizzy's work as it did on that of the aircrewmen and ground crews.

More and more Mosquitoes were being built, and Don Bennett was keen to get as many of them as he could to strengthen his Pathfinder Force. It was not long before 163 Squadron became fully operational with its proper quota of aircraft. Aircrews and others were drafted from various squadrons, some of them knowing very little about Mosquitoes. Many of the new maintenance men had worked on Wellingtons only. Tommy had to introduce the newly arrived navigators to a different style of work in readiness for LNSF operations. One Squadron Leader was sent up from the Central

Flying School to learn how the Pathfinders did things. The advice on navigation that Tom gave him was, 'Keep things simple.' Many years later, Sir Francis Chichester 'kept things simple' when he navigated his way around the world in his yacht!

Fresh pilots came with their own navigators sometimes. To all these entrants, Ivor and Tommy must have seemed like God's gift to operational flying in Mosquitoes. After all, they shared five DFCs between them, as well as a vast wealth of experience. Yet they did not rest on their laurels: they shared all the dangers and did their quota of sorties to Berlin and elsewhere.

Bill Jinks was a fresh-faced young pilot who had sailed from Avonmouth to Halifax, Nova Scotia, on the SS *Volendam* in December 1941 to serve with RAF Training Command. He had been retained in Canada for over two years despite constant pleading to be allowed to return to operational duties. Eventually, he had his request granted and he went on twenty-three missions with 163 Squadron in 1945. He remembers that Ivor and Tommy were regarded as 'Press-On Types', possibly the finest tribute that could be paid to Bomber Command aircrew by other fliers. Even hardened aircrew like Bill's navigator, who himself had been an evader after being shot down over the continent, had the highest regard for both Ivor and Tommy but, perhaps had a particular admiration for the professional way that Tommy dealt with navigational matters.

In *Clean Sweep*, a biographical tribute to Ivor's distinguished service, a nice compliment is paid to Tommy by Frank Lilley, a sergeant-navigator who was one of the earliest to join 163 Squadron. He described Tommy, a kind of father-figure, as a man who did wonders for the Squadron's comradeship. In the same vein, Bill Jinks remembers Tommy's kindness to young navigators who had been newly commissioned. It was typical of his thoughtfulness to take them under his wing. He not only introduced them to the ways of an Officers' Mess but, also, made himself available at all times to give advice and guidance. Bill had a clear recollection as well that Tommy was always at hand for drinks at the bar and ever ready to give personal tuition on a series of RAF songs (e.g., 'The Sha-i-bah Blues'), which, for reasons of respectability, cannot be quoted here.

Frank Lilley remembers how Tommy, who had worked his way

up through the ranks, could see through anyone who tried to take advantage of a young, trusting Commanding Officer. It was unusual, in service life, to have a man like Ivor in charge, for he still possessed a child-like innocence that was based on an unshakeable Christian faith. Yet he was not in any sense sanctimonious. He encouraged voluntary attendance at a Sunday afternoon church service, but he equally approved of the get-togethers at the monthly Squadron dances, with beer at 2d a pint. Both functions proved to be great Squadron morale boosters, and Bill Jinks recalls how Tommy was a prime mover at both occasions, singing on Sundays in fine voice, and invariably acting as Bar Officer. In fact, he administered four or five bars in different parts of the building, but whether the books balanced at the end of the evening was a matter for conjecture. What was certain was that because of Tommy's enthusiastic example, a good time would be had by all.

In a more restrained manner, Ivor's influence on the Squadron was such that his friendship was still treasured by those who had worked with him and flown with him, despite the passage of nearly sixty years.

Under Ivor's command, supported by Tommy's experience and loyalty, 163 Squadron went into action in their Canadian-built Mosquitoes. On 1 February they were at Berlin on a 'big do' according to an entry in Tommy's logbook. The two-wave attack with 122 aircraft was the largest Mosquito bombing raid on the capital. In the same month, there were successful raids on Hanover, Magdeburg and Berlin again. Unusually for the Flying Brooms, one operation had to be aborted because of a port engine failure. Altogether in February, 163 Squadron went over Berlin on twenty-four separate sorties. In March, Ivor and Tommy went back there twice. On 22 March as many as 142 Mosquitoes attacked Berlin in two waves, the largest Mosquito operation ever. Only one aircraft was lost. During March, only by happy coincidence of course, Tommy was able to supervise two flights to Whitchurch airfield (near Bristol) in an Airspeed Oxford.

On the night of 12 April, there was another concentrated two-wave attack on Berlin. Some aircraft were coned by searchlights and flak was fired, and a few fighters were spotted. However, it seemed as if the Germans were becoming not only exhausted by the constant bombing, but demoralised as well. It so happened that this was the last time that Ivor and Tommy flew together on a Berlin raid. The mission was summarised in an Intelligence Report thus:

ATTACK ON BERLIN (Second attack)

In accordance with instructions contained in Form B, No.631, 37 Mosquitoes took off; 36 attacked the primary target and 1 was abortive. 3 out of the 4 Oboe Mosquitoes successfully dropped markers by means of their Precision Device. These markers, however, began to fall 2 minutes early with the result that most of them were extinguished by the time the later of our aircraft arrived. Consequently the bombing, though quite good at first, tended to be scattered in the later stages of the attack. Some fires were seen in the built up area as a result of the previous attack. Defences: Slight heavy flak, with numerous searchlights coning.

On 17 April, Ivor and Tommy were not scheduled to fly to Berlin with 163 Squadron. Tommy, never one to miss an opportunity, left the station to honour a pre-arranged date. Ivor, as he normally did as Squadron Commander, went to wish the crews a safe trip before they took off. His words proved to be too much of a temptation to Fate, for one of the pilots lost his balance as he climbed into his Mosquito, tripped and twisted his ankle. He was declared unfit by the Medical Officer. Rather than have an aborted flight, Ivor took over and piloted the plane to Berlin with Sergeant John Brown as his navigator. When Tommy heard about it, he was furious that Ivor had 'sneaked' in an extra operation. Over the next hours and days, he pleaded with Ivor to grant him one more flight to Berlin, just to even the score, but his wish was not granted.

On 18 April, the Flying Brooms went on what was to be their final operation, a comparatively long flight to Schleiszheim near Munich. It was Tommy's fifty-eighth Mosquito sortie since he and Ivor had formed their partnership, but Ivor's fifty-ninth – a statistic that still irritated Tommy somewhat. However, he was happy enough when he went on leave two days later, and happier still a week or so after that when the news came through that on 30 April, Hitler had committed suicide in his Berlin bunker. On the night of 2 May, pilots of 163 Squadron took part in Bomber Command's last raid of the war when Kiel was attacked.

So, on 8 May 1945 (VE Day), the war in Europe came to an end after six years of misery, but of great camaraderie. The men and women of 163 Squadron, in sympathy with men and women all over Britain, rejoiced and celebrated, but in their happiness did not forget those friends they had lost on the way.

After a decent interval in which to recover from all the excitement, Ivor and Tommy flew in a Lancaster on what they described as 'Cook's Tours'. They took with them groups of ground crew, the people who had serviced their Mosquitoes conscientiously and efficiently for so many years. This gesture of gratitude and friendship was typical of the Flying Brooms' attitude towards their colleagues, no matter their rank or status. The low-level flights enabled the ground crews to observe at first-hand how the 'whirlwind had been reaped' as 'Bomber' Harris had predicted. On three separate trips, they went over Kaiserslautern, Karlsruhe, Mannheim, Frankfurt, Mainz, Koblenz, Remagen, Bonn, Cologne, Hanover, Osnabruck, Münster and the Ruhr towns where, no doubt, they saw the same horrific destruction that the author witnessed when he served as a conscript soldier in Germany after the war.

Despite the dreadful carnage inflicted upon them by the bombing campaign, many survived and, indeed, prospered in the cellars of their ruined homes in Düsseldorf (as in other cities). In the midst of the devastation, they showed a tremendous tenacity of spirit much to be admired. A happy circumstance of another kind was seen by the author in the ruins of Cologne. Though the railway station next door and the Rhine bridge nearby had been demolished, the twin spires of the cathedral still soared proudly into the skies and, where a cookie had landed nearby, a deep crater revealed a superb Roman mosaic that had been hidden for 1500 years perhaps.

Until the end of August 1945, Tommy continued to fly, though infrequently. His final flight with Ivor was on the last day of the month, but they were in the air for only twenty minutes, and in an Airspeed Oxford at that. On the final page of Tommy's logbook, it is recorded that since 1938, he had flown a total well in excess of 1000 hours, over 250 of them at night and, altogether, he had been on eighty-three operations against the enemy.

It was not until 26 September that Mrs Broom entered in her War

Diary that Tom's operational flying had ended. In the meantime, Tommy went through the process of reverting to civilian status. He had understood that he had been placed in Demobilisation Group 21, but his name was missing from the list. His original '9 and 3' contract had ended in 1944, so that his recorded war-time service would have begun then. Tommy had forgotten, also, that he had been granted a permanent commission when he had been promoted from the ranks. However, everything was sorted out eventually and Tommy obtained his release. It is amusing to note that Tommy's last meal in the RAF was eaten in the Officers' Mess at RAF Uxbridge where, in 1932, he had spent so many hours on fatigues scrubbing the place out.

By the end of November, Tom had left the RAF for the peace and tranquillity of Old Posset. When he got home to Rhondda Villas, he read a letter that his parents had received from the Clerk of the Urban District Council (better known to local residents as Arthur Reynolds or 'Mr Portishead'). Dated 6 November, the letter read:

Dear Mr and Mrs Broom,

At a meeting of the Council held last evening, reference was made to the additional award to your son, Squadron Leader T. Broom, and I was requested by the Council to convey to you the Council's congratulations on this additional award. From official citation there is no doubt that your son has earned the recognition which has been bestowed upon him and the Council has unanimously resolved to place on official record its appreciation of your son's service to his country.

In the issue of *Flight* dated 27 December, Tom's mother and father were able to read with immense pride the following citation:

The KING has been graciously pleased to approve the following award in recognition of gallantry and devotion to duty in the execution of air operations:-

Second Bar to Distinguished Flying Cross

Act. Sqn. Ldr. T.J. Broom, D.F.C., R.A.F. No. 163 Sqn.

This officer has a long and distinguished record of operational flying. He first flew against the enemy in September 1939, and since then he has completed a large number of day and night sorties against heavily defended targets in Germany. On one occasion he was forced to leave his aircraft by parachute and another time his aircraft crashed in occupied territory, but he evaded capture and returned to this country, where he resumed operational flying with undiminished enthusiasm. The sterling qualities of courage, leadership and devotion to duty displayed by Sqn. Ldr. Broom have materially contributed to the operational efficiency of each squadron with which he has served. In addition his work as Squadron navigation officer has been worthy of the highest praise.

This then was not so much an award to recognise one particular instance of courage and skill, but more of a tribute to Tommy's constant display of those qualities that define a hero. Yet, no matter how indefatigably active Tommy had been, he did not qualify for the Defence Medal that most servicemen received. It seems that he had not spent enough time on non-operational duties during his war-service! Now, however, the time had come for Tommy to opt for a quieter, more mundane life as a civilian, whereas the other Broom, Ivor, decided to make the RAF his life's career. This was to be a parting of the ways for the Flying Brooms, but not a separation, for their friendship was life-long. Ivor's name will crop up again and again in the remainder of this story, but as Air Marshal Sir Ivor Broom KCB, CBE, DSO, DFC**, AFC.

It is proper, and salutary, in the midst of this celebratory remembrance, to note and to mourn those 58,375 aircrew of Bomber Command who lost their lives during the 1939–45 War. Nor should we forget the thousands of soldiers, sailors, airmen, merchant seamen and civilians who did not survive to savour the relief and joy of the long awaited peace.

In his Clearance Certificate from the RAF, there was a statement to the effect that S/Ldr (51227) T.J. Broom had been cleared of all known charges in respect of deficiencies of public clothing and equipment, articles on equipment loan, or charge except for £0.0s.0d, which has been reported to Air Ministry Accounts 2(a).

CHAPTER SIXTEEN

Yesterday's Tomorrows

The few weeks that remained of 1945 gave Tom a little time in which to unwind and to consider, now that he was fast approaching his thirty-second birthday, what he should do with the rest of his life, and how he should set about it. Wisely, he gave himself six months to come to terms with civilian life after his thirteen years in the Air Force, during which he had experienced six years of war-time service when his life had been repeatedly put in jeopardy. Now he felt the need to renew acquaintance with those of his generation who had survived the years of conflict, who were also settling back into those quiet village routines that they appreciated more readily now than when they had been village lads growing up. It was with a feeling of deep gratitude that they enjoyed their good fortune, and they were more than happy to be able to reminisce about days gone by over a pint or two of beer. They favoured the 'Plough' as a meeting place, which, fortunately or otherwise, was almost opposite the Post Office where they could draw from their gratuity savings as required[12].

Around midday, therefore, Tom would be found in the 'Plough' chatting to one or other of his old cronies, perhaps 'Happy' Bessant (ex-Airborne), Cyril Smith (North Somerset Yeomanry), 'Jumbo' Wheeler (as Bob had been, with the Royal Tank Corps in the Middle East), Gilbert Payne and 'Hambone' Rollings (both with the Royal Artillery in North Africa), Geoff Hill (an ex-RSM with the Somerset Light Infantry), or Dick Cooling (Royal Navy). On one night of the week, Tom would meet Bernard Kristiansen, a very dear friend who had failed his medical examination for entry into the services, but who had contributed to the war by working at the Nail Factory producing, amongst other things, those metal screws for the RAF's Mosquitoes. Sometimes, Clem Manning (landlord of the 'Plough') and Bruce North (a tobacconist) would take a few of them to the races at Cheltenham where, very likely, they squandered even more of their money, but what relaxing excursions they were after the deprivations of the war, and how they rejoiced at being the 'Lucky Ones'. Cyril Smith (the husband of Peggy the Hairdresser) played the occasional game of rugby for Horfield Athletic and he persuaded Tom to play regularly during the winter months, though Tom was beginning to sense that physical activity of this kind was getting to be too much for him.

When Tom had had enough of this heady mixture of rehabilitation and celebration, he was obliged to reintroduce some discipline into his life. He was well aware that he had much to contribute and that his useful service was far from over. Therefore, when he read that men and women with experience were required to work in Germany, he applied to join the Control Commission, the organisation that had responsibility for bringing some semblance of normality into the lives of the defeated population in the British Zone of Occupied Germany. He obtained a 2½-year contract starting in June 1946 and was posted to Bad Salzuflien. It was a small spa town that had been largely untouched by the bombing campaign, even though it was situated between Minden in the north and Detmold to the south, and between Hanover in the east and Osnabruck to the west, an area of Germany not unknown to Tom – at least, from the skies above. It was ironic in the extreme that part of Tom's work now was to help with the rebuilding of a country that for the previous six years he had done his best to destroy. During his posting, he tackled various jobs, the chief of which was as Assistant Commandant helping to run the civil side of the town's affairs. Perhaps the biggest surprise he had in Bad Salzuflien was when somebody shouted out from a passing vehicle, 'Watch out Broomy!' Of course, as soon as he heard this style of address, Tom knew that the voice had to belong to a Posset man. The Jeep's driver was Tom Broad, a Major serving with the Royal Engineers.

Since he had never had the opportunity to study the language in his schooldays, Tom could not carry out a conversation in German, but as a functionary it was important for him to be able to communicate with the town's representatives. He was given the help of an interpreter, *Frau* Annemarie Haslinger, who had studied briefly in England just before the War. Originally from Mülheim in the Ruhr, she was an attractive twenty-nine-year-old widow with a six-year-old daughter, Sigrid. Whereas during the war Tom had kept well clear of marital commitments, now he soon fell head over heels for Annemarie and, eventually, she responded positively to his proposal of marriage. The wedding ceremony, in July 1948, was conducted at a local chapel by a minister of the Church of Scotland. Though by no means ungenerous by nature, Tom does remember with some pride that the celebrations (including the reception) only cost him £20!

When Tom's contract ended in December, the family moved to Portishead in 1949 to stay for a while with Mr and Mrs Broom at Rhondda Villas. There was no time to renew and to celebrate old friendships this time. Whereas Tom had had responsibilities of a general nature before, now he had a particular duty of care to two very special people who would need his support and protection in, what was to them, a foreign environment. Tom's first task was to find immediate and, if possible, permanent employment. He successfully applied for a clerical post with the Esso Petroleum Company at Avonmouth. This entailed an early departure from the house to catch the 7.30 a.m. bus from the village to take him as far as Pill, where he boarded the ferry to take him across the river Avon to Shirehampton on the Gloucestershire bank. On the Portway, he caught another bus that took him into Avonmouth in good time to start work at 9 o'clock. It was in 1950 that the author first made acquaintance with Tommy, when he caught the same bus to Pill and was ferried across the Avon in such good company. But Tommy never said a word about his past life, and it was only by accident, many years later, that his exploits became known.

Before long, Tom obtained a council-house tenancy in Channel View Crescent on the hill overlooking the village. It was here that their marriage was blessed by the birth of a baby daughter on 30 January 1950. She was christened Mary-Ann, a happily chosen name in honour of Annemarie. By now, of course, Sigrid was ten years old. She was clearly a girl of some ability, for in her final report from St Peter's Junior School in 1951, she came second in a class of forty-two children, and this despite the fact that just two years earlier her command of English had been quite elementary. Tom and Annemarie reasoned that it was essential for Sigrid to receive more personal attention and so, from the autumn of 1951 until the summer of 1956, she attended a small private school in Clevedon, the Wycliffe School, where the classes were sometimes as small as eight and hardly ever more than fifteen or so. She excelled at German (to be expected), French and Geography, the combination of subjects that she studied when she entered the Sixth Form at the Weston-super-Mare Grammar School for Girls, where she ended her schooldays as a Prefect showing 'initiative and intelligence'. From there, Sigrid went to the Commercial College in Bristol to acquire short-hand and typing skills. After that, she spent a year at Toulouse and another year in Munich teaching English before returning to London to work as a technical translator.

In general, the 1950s were years when life gradually returned to its routine of ordinary family activity, with its usual mixture of joys and sorrows. In February 1953, John Ashford Broom died aged seventy-four years, and he was buried in St Peter's churchyard not far from the home where he had spent all his married life. As part of her grieving, Mrs Broom dwelt on her memories of childhood and girlhood. One day, Tom hired a car to take his mother back to see the house in which she had been born and brought up. It was her first and only visit since she had left half-a-century before.

As well as the really important happenings, there were plenty of trivial occurrences, largely forgotten, that sometimes resurface from the depths of memory. In the early 1950s, various foods were still in short supply, and some shopkeepers, in true Thatcherite style, took advantage of the market situation to increase their profit margins. The government of the day used to emphasise the importance of certain foods like milk, orange juice and cod-liver-oil for growing children. A familiar slogan of the time was 'an egg for a child'. Once when Tom went shopping, the grocer claimed that he had no eggs available. When he heard this, Tom wasted no time and said, 'I see. So much for the Ministry of Food and its promises. I'm going to write to that blasted Minister to complain that he's failed to keep you properly supplied,' whereupon the grocer suddenly remembered that he had half-a-dozen eggs to spare from under the counter. So Mary-Ann, at least, had more than her proper ration of eggs that week!

Towards the end of the decade, an Air Ministry notice was published to the effect that Tom was no longer liable to be recalled into the Services as he had reached his forty-fifth birthday. Tom's commission was relinquished on 22 January 1959, but he was authorised to retain his honorary rank of Squadron Leader, a title to which he has the right to be addressed to this day.

In 1961, the family moved a little way down the hill, closer to the village, to make a new home for themselves at Mount Villa on Stoney Steep (or, as it was more familiarly known, Welley Bottom – believed to be an Old Posset rendering of Well Hay.) In 1961, also, Mary-Ann left St Barnabas Junior School to attend the Grammar School at Nailsea after achieving a successful 11+ examination result.

Though the new decade started most promisingly, within two years of moving into their new home, tragedy struck. One weekend at the beginning of May 1963, Annemarie complained that she was feeling a little unwell. When she showed no sign of recovery, her doctor sent her to Ham Green Hospital for observation but, in less than a week, she had died of acute hepatitis. She was only forty-six years old, and she and Tom had enjoyed together but fifteen years of fulfilling marriage. She was laid to rest in St Peter's churchyard, in a plot far away from her native land, but close to her loving family.

This shocking experience almost unbalanced Tom, but now he had to show courage of a different kind and a steadfastness that befitted his position as a young schoolgirl's father. Immediately after the funeral, Mary-Ann was taken to Germany for a brief stay with Annemarie's family. This gave her an opportunity to recover a little of her composure and it gave Tom, also, some space in which to grieve. Sigrid herself was shattered by her loss, but demonstrated her character when she voiced her intention to give up her career to look after Mary-Ann and Tom. Tom managed to convince her that he could cope and that, in any case, he could not possibly allow her to make such a sacrifice, so Sigrid reluctantly returned to London to continue with her work as an interpreter and translator.

It was a devastating loss for Mary-Ann to lose her mother, but to be deprived of her loving support at her tender age was particularly cruel. Tom was fortunate that he had a sister of Muriel's calibre.

From the time that Annemarie died, Muriel willingly acted as a substitute parent to Mary-Ann, and was always ready to be a chaperone whenever Tom felt that he needed a break. Tom was fortunate, also, that he had a kind and understanding neighbour in Myrtle Jelley who was prepared to counsel on women's matters at a crucial time in Mary-Ann's life. Of course, Tom himself did all he could to lighten the burden of her grief, and he made a point of taking her on regular outings to the cinema, the theatre, the zoo and the museum, and most summers he organised seaside trips for her.

In June 1965, the family had more cause for sadness when Tom's mother died aged eighty-four years, some twenty years after her eldest son had been returned safe and sound to her. Louise Broom was buried by her husband's side at St Peter's Church. This was a further harsh experience for Mary-Ann, so as soon as possible, and as a kind of compensation, Tom took her on a hastily arranged flight to Paris. Once there, he could not resist the temptation to board a train at the Gare d'Austerlitz bound for St Jean de Luz, where twenty-five years earlier he had rested briefly before crossing the Pyrenees to freedom.

They did not reach their destination until very late in the evening, so they went to the nearest restaurant to make some inquiries. They were advised that a lady who lived just across the road was usually quite happy to provide bed and board for chance visitors. Fortunately, there were rooms available for Mary-Ann and Tom. At the breakfast table the following morning they carried on a conversation as well as they could. The woman of the house was curious why the two of them had travelled to St Jean de Luz, for it was not normally thought of as a holiday resort by foreigners. Tom mentioned his previous visit in 1942, and of how Albert Johnson, Florentino and a young girl had helped him and his companions to escape across the Pyrenees. The woman jumped up from the table and dashed upstairs. When she returned, she handed over a slightly faded photograph of a young blonde girl wheeling a bicycle. She asked Tom if that was the young girl he had in mind. Tom was astounded but managed to splutter that indeed she was and that he would dearly love to see her again so that he could thank her properly. 'That's me,' she shrieked triumphantly, 'that's me!' Of course, from then on they were treated like royalty, and they left St Jean de Luz with much regret when the time came for them to depart.

In the summer of 1967, after spending a year in the Sixth Form at Nailsea, Mary-Ann decided to seek work, and she easily obtained a position with the Legal and General Insurance Company in Bristol. She was very happy there, but when the branch was relocated in 1972 to the towering Robinsons' building by Bristol Bridge, its open-plan system did not suit Mary-Ann's temperament. With her manager's support, she was immediately employed at the more intimate Provincial Insurance office in the centre of the city. It was in 1967, also, that Sigrid made a significant move. She went to Montreal to act as an interpreter at the World Fair – Expo 67. She worked in particular at the Tunisian Centre where she was photographed standing alongside President Bourguiba.

Sigrid was so impressed with Canada that she decided to settle there. In fact, she lives to the south of the Canadian border at Vermont in the USA where she now runs a small estate agency as well as the Sugar Bush Skiing Centre. Every now and then she returns to Portishead to see Tom and Mary-Ann and to join in family celebrations.

In the very same year, 1967, Tom left the Esso office in Avonmouth to join the Brake Lining Company at Queen's Square in Bristol to look after the firm's accounts. This enabled him to leave later in the morning and to be home a little earlier in the evening, so that he was able to spend rather more precious time in Mary-Ann's company. By now, Muriel (after much nagging by Tom on her behalf, and many a heated debate with the Town Council in the shape of Arthur Reynolds) had obtained the tenancy of a refurbished house in Coombe Avenue. There were plans to demolish Rhondda Villas to make way for a roundabout by the entrance to Slade Road School. The houses were demolished but thankfully, as far as children's safety was concerned, the Council had second thoughts concerning the roundabout.

By the end of the 1960s, Tom and Mary-Ann had learned to cope with their sorrows, and had good cause to welcome the new decade. In 1973, Tom celebrated Mary-Ann's engagement and marriage to Greg Iles, a local young man who, to Tom's delight, was quite an accomplished cricketer and footballer. It was in 1973, also, that Tom changed his job once more to become a clerical officer with the Post Office (British Telecom) at Queen Charlotte Street in Bristol. He stayed with them until 1979 when he retired to make the most of his remaining years, and this he insisted on despite being urged most strongly to stay on. In the meantime, in 1976, he had received the glad news that his old friend, Ivor Broom, was to be knighted – an occasion worthy to be toasted with many a pint.

Tom's sister, Muriel, decided to retire in 1979 as well. Apart from her war-time employment at the Bristol Aeroplane Company's underground factory at Corsham, she had worked all her life at Osmond and Tovey's drapery shop in the High Street, where her father had also worked. She was remembered with affection by the author's wife who was a regular customer at the shop when the children were growing up. Miss Broom, as she was known to us, never failed to ask after the children's well-being and seemed to rejoice at their various successes. Sadly, Muriel's retirement lasted but four months, and in June she was buried in the family grave at St Peter's at the age of sixty-seven years.

Tom's aim in his retirement was to keep his body active and his brain ticking over. He derived his greatest pleasure from seeing his grandsons developing into fine young men. At the time of writing, James is thirty years old. After graduating from Portsmouth University, he obtained a post with the IBM group. He has played cricket for the Gordano Valley XI, and football for one of the Portishead teams. Robert, two years younger than James, studied Marketing at Southampton University and now works for Lloyds TSB Bank. He plays cricket for Portishead, and captains the village team at the time of writing. Thus the two of them are maintaining the long-standing family sporting tradition. As the writer well knows, Tom is a very busy man, and is not readily available at home. There is nothing that he likes better than walking through the village meeting old friends, usually on his way to the 'Poacher' (the 'Anchor' that was) to have a drink and a chat with Bert Metcalf (who served in the Royal Navy during the war) and other friends. There is often much gentle banter between them about the seniority or the elan of whichever Service happens to be under discussion. Tom is frequently sought to speak at private functions and, altogether, he has addressed about twenty different organisations in the locality.

He is a loyal member of the Portishead branch of the Royal British Legion and has served in his time as its most distinguished President. Seldom is he absent from the Legion's monthly meetings, and if his apologies have to be given, more than likely he is away from the village visiting his old Pathfinder friends. He was a frequent guest at Sir Ivor and Lady Jess's home in Berkshire, where he was regarded as one who belonged to the family, a sort of brother as well as a dear companion. Sometimes, his visits coincided with the arrival of other old colleagues. If not, Tommy was quite prepared to travel further afield each year to renew and refresh those friendships that were, and still are, so important to him. In fact, the author acknowledges with envy almost, but certainly with admiration, the steadfastness of their comradeship, a companionship tested under stress well over sixty years ago and tempered by mutual respect ever since.

In May 1984, after some coaxing from Sir Ivor, Tom (or rather, Tommy once more) attended his first Pathfinder Dinner at RAF Wyton. It was a delight to reminisce with such fine people, but what made the occasion especially memorable was the presence of the 'Great Don' himself. After this, Tommy maintained contact by attending various Pathfinder and Bomber Command functions. These meetings with his fellow airmen of long ago featured more and more in his life, and indeed assumed greater significance as each year went by. They were all growing old together, and year by year they had cause to mourn the passing of many comrades. They became very much aware of the possibility of imminent parting, much more so than in their younger hectic days together, but the knowledge strengthened the bonds of friendship between them, and they cherished each other's company all the more.

In 1985, Tom left Stoney Steep for a basement flat in Adelaide Terrace, close to where his mother had worked as a maid, and within a three-minute walk of the Portishead cricket ground where he spends many a contented hour. But 1985 is fresh in Tom's memory for another reason. At the Pathfinder Dinner in May, Queen Elizabeth the Queen Mother graced the day with her presence, and Tom is very proud of the photograph that shows him standing next to Her Majesty. She was at RAF Wyton to meet the

Pathfinders forty years on from the end of the war. She had honoured the station once before, in 1943, when she had accompanied her husband, King George VI, to Wyton to inspect the Pathfinder squadrons.

When the Pathfinders marched together at the Cenotaph Ceremony on Armistice Sunday, their comradeship was displayed in more sombre fashion. Yet, though the occasion was one for sober reflection, there was still happiness, even merriment, when they repaired to the RAF Club in Piccadilly to share an 'Aircrew Breakfast' of bacon and eggs (with all the trimmings these days), followed by animated conversation in the bar. Year by year there has been an inevitable drop in the number of men and women who participate in these sad, but joyous, reunions. They come each succeeding year to pay tribute to the thousands of young men who paid for victory with their lives, who were never to see the dawning of brighter days.

Perhaps nothing gave Tom more pride and pleasure than being able to introduce Sir Ivor and Lady Jess to his friends in Old Posset. In 1989, for example, the two of them attended a Thanksgiving Dinner and Dance organised by the Portishead branch of the Royal British Legion to acknowledge the fiftieth anniversary of the War's beginning. The toast of 'Absent Friends' was given by Squadron Leader Tommy Broom and that to the 'Royal British Legion and the RAF Association' by Air Marshal Sir Ivor Broom – a most happy reunion of the Flying Brooms. Further visits were made in 1991 to celebrate the 70th Anniversary of the Royal British Legion, and in 1995, not only to pay tribute to Tom's Presidency of the Portishead branch in his last year of office, but also to celebrate the 50th Anniversary of the War"s end. Then in 1995 there was considerable excitement when Sir Ivor was the man honoured in the television series 'This Is Your Life'. Tommy, of course, was delighted to have the opportunity to praise (and to embarrass?) his friend.

At the 1997 Pathfinder Dinner at RAF Wyton (the only Pathfinder airfield still in use), the Patron of the Association, Ly Bennett, made a particularly delightful speech in which she rejoiced that growing old, and neither hearing nor seeing so clearly, had advantages. She only heard the nice things and, as far as she was able to judge, each gallant officer present still looked like an Adonis. As if to prove to her that they were as young as ever, Tommy and Bertie 'The Boy' Boulter went to Swanton Morley once more, where Bertie's Stearman (a US trainer aircraft) was stored. They wheeled it out of its hangar, checked it, and then flew it around the Norwich area for a while. Of course, this was legitimately done, for Bertie was regularly examined to test his fitness and 'airworthiness', but what a nerve at a combined age well in excess of 150 years. It is good to report that the exercise was repeated in 1998, 1999 and 2000.

'The Boy' is known to his friends as the man who baled out twice, and both in unusual circumstances. In 1944, his aircraft was badly shot up over Stuttgart, but by skilful piloting he managed to keep it aloft until the Channel was reached. He and his navigator abandoned their Mosquito over Dunkirk and parachuted to safety. In January 1945 when Bertie had to bale out for the second time, it was over England in supposedly friendly territory. Again, he landed safely. He knocked at the first house he came to and asked politely if he could use the telephone to contact his RAF base. He was told very sharply that there was a public phone-box just half-a-mile down the road!

Another annual get-together that Tom used to look forward to was his visit to Criccieth to stay with his friend from the 1940s, George Forbes (of Abersoch fame and much else). Once there, Tom and George would go to Manchester to see Roy Ralston, their dear old squadron commander and friend. Invariably they would patronise a local pub in the evening to reminisce. Roy suffered a severe stroke when he was comparatively young, at sixty-two years of age, but he bore with his misfortune cheerfully until he died in his eighties in 1996.

It is sad to report that since this book's first edition was published, Tommy's fine companion Sir Ivor died on 24 January 2003 and was buried on 4 February, the very day that George Forbes died. Despite these grievous losses, with Lady Jess's gracious care the old Pathfinder friends still meet together regularly. In 2005 and 2006, the writer was privileged to attend their get-togethers, first to pay respect to the memory of Sir Ivor at his graveside in Little Rissington, and then to refresh acquaintance over a meal at a local inn.

On 3 May 2006, Lady Jess attended a special get-together at the

Folk Hall in Portishead to witness the presentation by Tom to the Town Council of 'Home Run' (a print of an original painting by Gerald Coulson). The print had been signed by Tom and Sir Ivor.

Tom continues to live life to its full, and he will continue to rejoice in the company of his family and his numerous comrades.

One hopes that the sun will be shining in Mary-Ann's garden on 22 January 2014 so that a hundreth birthday photograph may be taken to add to Tom's portfolio.

Notes

1. For the benefit of younger readers perhaps it would be as well to explain that mensuration meant the ability to measure areas, distances, volumes and weights. Before the metric system was introduced into Britain, schoolchildren had to be proficient in the four rules of Arithmetic, with special emphasis on multiplication tables in order to cope with calculations necessary to change pounds to shillings, pence and farthings (x20, x12, x4), to change miles to furlongs, chains, yards, feet and inches (x8, x10, x22, x3, x12), to change tons to hundredweights, quarters, stones, pounds and ounces (x20, x4, x2, x14, x16) and to change gallons into quarts and pints (x4, x2).

2. Dixie Dean had been badly injured in a motorcycle accident, so much so that a metal plate had been inserted in his skull to protect him from further injury. It was no wonder, therefore, that he became known as the best header of a football in the game! He was, also, a gifted player whose record of goal-scoring still holds despite the passage of seventy years and more. In the 1927–1928 season, he scored sixty goals in thirty-nine league games. During his career with Everton from 1925 until 1937, he scored 349 goals in 399 games.

3. In the first half of the twentieth century, the British Empire covered a quarter of the world's land surface. The Empire girded the globe eastward from Britain to the Mediterranean and Africa, to India, Malaysia, Australia and New Zealand, the Pacific Islands, to Canada and back to Britain. There were Dominions, Colonies, Protectorates and Mandated Territories, all supervised from London and reigned over by the King Emperor. It was properly claimed that the sun never set on the Empire.

4. The British were unwelcome because Omdurman had been the scene of a massacre in 1898 when the Dervishes led by the Khalifa Abdullah (the Mahdi's successor) had been crushed by Kitchener's force, comprising about 25,000 armed troops, supported by howitzers and machine-guns and with several gunboats anchored in the Nile. The charging Dervishes were mown down, and by the time the one-sided battle had ended, though there had been one or two Dervish successes, 10,000 of them lay dead with another 20,000 wounded or captured as prisoners-of-war. This attack on the Dervishes was intended, in a way, to be a punishment of the Sudanese rebels (commanded by Muhammad al-Mahdi) who had killed General Gordon (a great English hero) at the siege of Khartoum in 1885. It is interesting to note that Kitchener a little later managed to embitter the Boers as well, when over 25,000 women and children died in the concentration camps set up by him to quell the Dutch colonials.

5. The Khamsin is a hot, dry wind that blows across the Sahara Desert towards the Mediterranean in the first half of the year. As it blows it dries up everything that it touches, and picks up vast amounts of sand and dust, which can endanger the lives of people caught unawares. Khamsin is the Arabic word for fifty and the Khamsin wind is so called for it blows for about fifty days each year. In the desert battles of the Second World War, a Khamsin was the only thing that could bring everything to a halt.

6. Mrs Mollison was better known as Amy Johnson. Born in Hull, she was possibly the most famous and popular Englishwoman of the 1930s. She was the first woman to fly solo from England to Australia in her aircraft Jason in 1930. In 1931 she flew to Japan and back and in 1932 made a record solo flight to Cape Town and back. In 1936 she set a new record flight from London to Cape Town. Tragically, she lost her life in 1941 when she had to bale out over the Thames estuary when carrying out war work.

7. C.W.A. Scott and Tom Campbell Black had won the England to Australia Air Race in 1934 flying a de Havilland Comet DH88, a specially designed and built twin-engined monoplane with an all-wood construction. One of the other two de Havilland racers was flown by Amy and Jim Mollison. Scott and Black flew from Maidenhall, Suffolk, and reached Australia after covering 11,323 miles in just over seventy-one hours to win the first prize of £10,000. The Comet DH88 was the forerunner of the Mosquito that Tom was to navigate with distinction in the coming war.

8. The day's routine in the Sudan was quite different from that on a station in England. Tom would be woken by a Sudanese servant at 5.15 a.m. with a cup of tea and a cake. Work started at 6 a.m. and continued until it was time for breakfast at 8 a.m. After an hour's break, it was back to work until midday when there would be a light meal (tiffin) of soup and salad, perhaps. This would be followed by a cool shower and undisturbed rest until 4 p.m. When the 'siesta' was over, and after another cool shower, dinner was served at 5.30 p.m. except for those airmen involved in sporting activities. They were able to dine separately – once the sun had set and play had to end. The sports pitches were kept in good condition as they were regularly watered from the irrigation ditches. Cricket matches were usually played on Sundays from 7 a.m. until 10 a.m. and from 4 p.m. until it got too dark at 6 p.m. The heat at midday was just too oppressive with temperatures ranging from 105 to 125 degrees Fahrenheit. Many of the Sudan's British officials (civilian colonials) were Oxbridge graduates and some of them were more than useful cricketers. Unfortunately, they invariably provided the opposition when Tom opened the innings for RAF Khartoum. Though he was pretty competent, Tom could not perform as brilliantly as J.W. Seamer (Oxford University and Somerset) who scored a century before breakfast! Tom remembers, with pleasure really, that he dropped Seamer when he was on 98, but then caught him at mid-on for 101. (In his book Bedside Cricket, Christopher Martin-Jenkins told this story as related to him by Seamer himself. It seems that, in 1998, Jake Seamer was as hale and hearty as Tom was.)

9. In August 1937, Amelia Earhart, the American heroine-aviator, landed at Khartoum on her ill-fated attempt at a round-the-world flight. She had been the first woman to fly solo across the Atlantic in 1932 and across the Pacific in 1935, and she broke several records in flights around America. She received numerous awards in recognition of her feats and was adored by the American people. She hoped, now, to become the first woman to fly around the world and the first aviator to do so at the Equator (the longest round-the-world route). On 21 May 1937, she left California (with her navigator) in her Lockheed Electra, crossed the jungles of Brazil, the deep waters of the South Atlantic, and then braved the sandstorms of Africa before reaching Khartoum. From there, she continued to India, Malaya, Singapore, the islands of the East Indies, Darwin in Australia and then New Guinea. She left there on 2 July but, though a radio message was received from her, no trace has ever been found of the brave woman, her navigator or the aeroplane. People all over the world mourned the loss of Amelia Earhart.

10. The Vickers Wellington, affectionately nicknamed 'Wimpey' had been designed by the famous Barnes Wallis to a geodetic design (a sort of basket-weave) that enabled it to survive quite severe damage. It could carry a 4500-pound bomb load at a speed of 250 mph. It was too slow really to be used on daylight raids into Germany.

11. Altogether, Dedee de Jongh made three dozen trips through France and across the Pyrenees into Spain in her determination to help British and Allied airmen to gain their freedom. She was arrested by the Gestapo on suspicion of being a French patriot and was imprisoned for a year before being sent to a concentration camp. She survived because of her resolute spirit, and was awarded the George Medal as a tribute to her great courage. When the war ended, she trained as a nurse, to work in a leper colony in Africa – yet another measure of her courageous humanity.

12. All servicemen and women who had served in the Armed Forces during the War were entitled to a gratuity, a nominal sum of money to finance their return to ordinary life. In addition, demobilised personnel were given a suit of clothes with accessories (hats, shoes, etc.). For some years the 'demob-suit' was a source of merriment or embarrassment to all and sundry, for more often than not it was badly tailored and ill-fitting.

Appendix I

Record of Service

Dates	RAF stations
5/32–11/32	Uxbridge
11/32–4/35	40(B) Squadron Abingdon
4/35–9/35	Air Armament School Eastchurch
9/35–1/36	Central Flying School Upavon
1/36–11/37	47(B) Squadron Khartoum (Sudan)
11/37–9/38	6(B) Squadron Ismailia (Egypt), Ramleh and Semakh (Palestine)
10/38–1/39	Air Observer & Gunnery School Leconfield and Aldergrove
1/39– 11/40	105(B) Squadron Harwell, Reims and Villeneuve (France), Watton and Swanton Morley
11/40–1/42	13 Operational Training Unit Bicester
1/42–8/42	105(B) Squadron HORSHAM St Faith and Marham
8/42– 5/44	1655 Mosquito Training Unit Marham, Finmere and Warboys
5/44–9/44	571(B) Squadron Oakington
9/44–1/45	128(B) Squadron Wyton
1/45–9/45	163(B) Squadron Wyton

Record of Operational Duty In France

Squadron	Aircraft	No. of Sorties
105 Squadron	Fairey Battle	2

In England

Squadron	Aircraft	No. of Sorties
105 Squadron	Bristol Blenheim	15
105 Squadron	DH Mosquito	8
571 Squadron	DH Mosquito	34
128 Squadron	DH Mosquito	16
163 Squadron	DH Mosquito	8

Grand Total of Sorties 83

Operational Periods

9/39–11/40

2/42–8/42

5/44–5/45

Aircraft in which Tommy Flew

Airspeed Oxford

Avro Anson and Lancaster (Mk III)

Bristol Blenheim (I, IV) and Bisley

de Havilland Tiger Moth and Mosquito (I, III, IV,XVI, XX)

Fairey Gordon, Gordon Floatplane and Battle

Handley Page Heyford

Hawker Hart and Hardy

Miles Master

Vickers Valentia, Vincent and Wellington (III)

Tommy's Map of
Operations

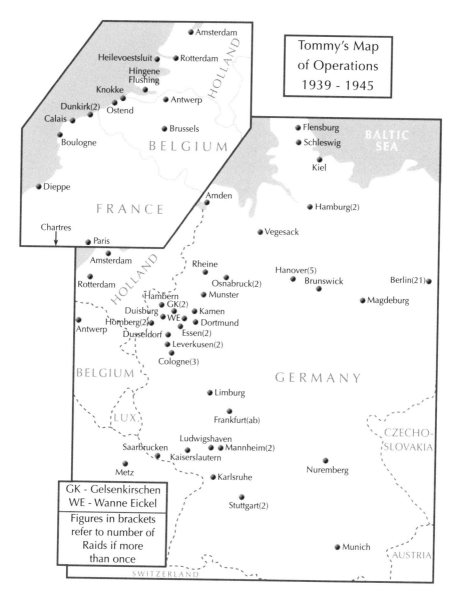

Tommy's Map
of Operations
1939 - 1945

● Amsterdam
Heilevoestsluit ● ● Rotterdam
Hingene
Flushing
Knokke ●
Dunkirk(2) ● Ostend
Calais ●
Boulogne
● Antwerp
● Brussels
BELGIUM
HOLLAND

● Flensburg
● Schleswig
BALTIC SEA
Kiel

● Dieppe
FRANCE
Amden
● Hamburg(2)

Chartres
↓ ● Paris
● Vegesack

Amsterdam
● Rotterdam
HOLLAND
Hambern
Duisburg ● GK(2)
Homberg(2) ● ● WE
Antwerp ● Dusseldorf
Rheine ●
Osnabruck(2)
● Munster
● Kamen
● Dortmund
Essen(2)
● Leverkusen(2)
Cologne(3)
Hanover(5)
● Brunswick
Berlin(21) ●
● Magdeburg

BELGIUM
LUX.
● Limburg
GERMANY

Frankfurt(ab)
CZECHO-
SLOVAKIA

Ludwigshaven
Saarbrucken ● ● Mannheim(2)
● Kaiserslautern
Metz
● Karlsruhe
Nuremberg ●

GK - Gelsenkirschen
WE - Wanne Eickel

Figures in brackets
refer to number of
Raids if more
than once

Stuttgart(2)

● Munich
AUSTRIA

SWITZERLAND

Brief Notes

The various branches of the Services had their own coats of arms and mottoes – their badges and battle cries. Those relevant to Tommy's service were:

Royal Air Force: *Per ardua ad astra*
  (By steep and toilsome ways to the stars)

Bomber Command: Strike hard strike sure

Pathfinders: We guide to strike

105 Squadron: *Fortis in praeliis* (Valiant in battles)

571 Squadron: *Facta non versa* (Action not words)

128 Squadron: *Fuliminis instar* (Like a thunderbolt)

Tommy served with 105 Squadron from January 1939 until November 1940 (a period that included the disastrous Battle of France and the low-level attacks on the Channel ports to destroy the invasion barges). In both of these actions the squadron suffered severe losses, and surely proved itself worthy of its motto. Tommy again served with 105 Squadron from January 1942 until November 1942. In fact, 105 Squadron carried out more raids than any other Bomber Command squadron. It was the first squadron to be equipped with Mosquitoes, and it made the first daylight raid on Berlin on 30 January 1943. One of its Commanding Officers was W/Cdr Hughie Edwards who won his Victoria Cross in 1941. With the development of the Pathfinder Force, 105 Squadron became an Oboe squadron.

During his career as a navigator, Tommy flew with 118 different pilots, most of them when they were attending training courses at 13 OTU at Bicester or 1655 MTU at Marham, Finmere and Warboys. Some of the pilots subsequently became quite well known, many of them earning awards for gallantry. Amongst Tommy's pilots were:

Sgt Swan, the first to climb to 30,000 feet in a Mosquito, who then crashed through a hedge on landing!

F/O Downs belly-landed a Mosquito with its bomb load still on board.

S/Ldr Darling DFC was on the Berlin raid that upset Goebbels, but was shot down.

W/Cdr Shand DFC, after making a name for himself as a low-level pilot, was shot down on his first sortie with the LNSF.

F/O Barber took part in the 1000th Mosquito sortie – on Taranto harbour.

F/O Monaghan was on the raid on Amiens jail that enabled French patriots to escape execution by the Germans.

S/Ldr Parry DSO, DFC was on the raid on Gestapo Headquarters in Oslo, as was F/O Bristow DFC who was shot down on a later operation.

G/Capt Kyle was reputed to be the finest of all Station Commanders.

W/Cdr Ralston DSO, DFM was a brilliant low-level attacker and, with Ivor Broom, was one of the finest leaders that airmen could serve with.

Tommy formed a few regular partnerships. He flew with F/Lt Barley fifteen times; with F/Lt Lascelles sixteen times; with S/Ldr Duncan twenty times; with F/O Tootal eighteen times (including two operations); with S/Ldr Costello-Bowen 156 times (including twenty-three operations); and with W/Cdr Broom 121 times (including fifty-eight operations with one aborted).

During the war, the RAF suffered some 86,000 losses altogether. Approximately 58,500 were from Bomber Command, 9000 from Coastal Command, 7500 from Fighter Command and as many as 11,000 men and women lost their lives during periods of training. Of the Bomber Command deaths, 3500 were Pathfinders.

Whereas, in peacetime, promotion through the ranks had been a comparatively slow process, so many lives were lost in the war that it was found necessary to promote men of experience and proven leadership rapidly.

Ranks in the RAF

AC2 – Aircraftman 2nd Class

AC1 – Aircraftman 1st Class

LAC – Leading Aircraftman

Cpl – Corporal

Sgt – Sergeant

F/Sgt – Flight Sergeant

W/O – Warrant Officer

P/O – Pilot Officer

F/O – Flying Officer

F/Lt – Flight Lieutenant

S/Ldr – Squadron Leader

W/Cdr – Wing Commander

G/Capt – Group Captain

A/Comm – Air Commodore

Air Vice-Marshal

Air Marshal

Air Chief Marshal

Marshal of the Royal Air Force

Honours Awarded to Airmen

VC –Victoria Cross

DSO – Distinguished Service Order

DFC – Distinguished Flying Cross

DFM – Distinguished Flying Medal

AFC – Air Force Cross

The George Cross and the George Medal, though usually awarded to civilians, could be won in certain circumstances by Service men and women. If awarded the same decoration on more than one occasion, a bar or clasp would be worn on the original medal ribbon. In addition, of course, airmen who achieved high rank were further rewarded with, what could be termed, social honours.

Appendix IV

Places to Visit

City of Norwich Aviation Museum, Horsham St Faith
Norfolk & Suffolk Aviation Museum, Flixton, Suffolk
RAF Museum, Duxford, near Cambridge
Tangmere Aviation Museum, Chichester, Sussex
RAF Museum, Hendon, London
Public Record Office, Kew, London

Bibliography

Armitage, Michael, *The Royal Air Force*, Arms & Armour Press, London, 1993

Belsey, James and Reid, Helen, *West At War*, Redcliffe Press, Bristol, 1990

Bennett, D.C.T., *Pathfinder*, Frederick Muller, London, 1958

Blunt, Barry, *571 Mosquito Bomber Squadron*, Hattersley High School, Hyde, 1992

Bowman, Martin, *The Men Who Flew The Mosquito*, Patrick Stephens, Yeovil, 1995

Brickhill, Paul, *The Dam Busters*, Pan Books, London, 1954

Brown, Bryan and Loosley, John, *The Book Of Portishead*, Barracuda Books, Buckingham, 1982

Chorley, W.R., *Bomber Command Losses:1939–1940*, Midland Counties Publications, 1992

Collier, Richard, *1940 – The World In Flames*, Penguin, Harmondsworth, 1980

Deighton, Len, *Blood, Tears And Folly*, Pimlico, London, 1995

Dike, John, *Bristol Blitz Diary*, Redcliffe Press, Bristol, 1982

Gilbert, Martin, *Second World War*, Phoenix Press, London, 2000

Hawkins, Mac, *Somerset At War 1939–1945*, Dovecote Press, Wimborne, 1988

Joslin, John, *Old Posset and More Old Posset*, White Tree Books, Bristol, 1987 and 1988

Martin-Jenkins, C., *Bedside Cricket*, Book Club Associates, London, 1981

Mondey, David, *British Aircraft of World War 2*, Chancellor Press, London, 1995

Nesbit, Roy C., *The RAF in Camera 1903–1939*, Sutton Publishing/PRO, Stroud, 1995

Overy, Richard, *The Battle of Britain*, Penguin Books, London, 2004

Richards, Denis, *The Hardest Victory*, Penguin Books, London, 2001

Scott, Stuart, *Battle-Axe Blenheims*, Sutton Publishing, Littlehampton, 1997

Sharp, Martin and Bowyer, Michael, *Mosquito*, Grey Books, London, 1995

(NB In this book, Tommy is recorded as two people, Broom and Broome – and no wonder considering how busy he had been in the war!)

Shirer, William, *The Rise & Fall Of The Third Reich*, Pan Books, London, 1965

Smith, Godfrey, *How it was in the War*, Past Times, London, 1989

Spooner, Tony, *Clean Sweep*, Crecy Books, Midsomer Norton, 1994

Terraine, John, *The Right of the Line*, Wordsworth Editions, Ware, 1998

Warne, F.G., *The Bombing Of Bristol*, F.G. Warne, Bristol, 1943

Wigan, Eve, *The Tale Of Gordano*, Wessex Press, Taunton, 1950

Wilmot, Chester, *The Struggle For Europe*, Wordsworth Editions, Ware, 1997

Index